Lent and Easter Reflections
Catholic Daily Reflections Series

Lent and Easter Reflections
Catholic Daily Reflections Series

By
John Paul Thomas

My Catholic Life! Inc.
www.mycatholic.life

Copyright © 2016 by My Catholic Life! Inc. All rights reserved. www.mycatholic.life

Updated: 2021 with additional reflections.

Excerpts from the *Lectionary for Mass for Use in the Dioceses of the United States of America, second typical edition* © 2001, 1998, 1997, 1986, 1970 Confraternity of Christian Doctrine, Inc., Washington, DC. Used with permission. All rights reserved. No portion of this text may be reproduced by any means without permission in writing from the copyright owner.

Excerpts for Divine Mercy Sunday are taken from: *Divine Mercy in My Soul: Diary of Saint Maria Faustina Kowalska*, Marian Press, English Edition Copyright © 1987 Congregation of Marians of the Immaculate Conception, Eden Hill, Stockbridge, MA 01262. All rights reserved.

ISBN-10: 1533083711

ISBN-13: 978-1533083715

Dedication

To our Blessed Mother, who walked by her Son as He endured His Passion. May she walk by us every day, helping us carry the cross we have been given so that we, too, may be privileged to share in the joy of and glory in the Resurrection for all eternity.

By
John Paul Thomas

"John Paul Thomas" is the pen name this priest has chosen in honor of the Apostles Saints John and Thomas and the great evangelist Saint Paul. This name also evokes the memory of the great Pope Saint John Paul II.

John is the beloved Apostle who sought out a deeply personal and intimate relationship with his Savior. Hopefully the writings in this book point us all to a deeply personal and intimate relationship with our God. May John be a model of this intimacy and love.

Thomas is also a beloved Apostle and close friend of Jesus but is well known for his lack of faith in Jesus' Resurrection. Though he ultimately entered into a profound faith, crying out "my Lord and my God," he is given to us as a model of our own weakness of faith. Thomas should inspire us to always return to faith when we realize we have doubted.

As a Pharisee, Paul severely persecuted the early Christian Church. However, after going through a powerful conversion, he went on to become the great evangelist to the gentiles, founding many new communities of believers and writing many letters contained in Sacred Scripture. His letters are deeply personal and reveal a shepherd's heart. Paul is a model for all as we seek to embrace our calling to spread the Gospel.

Table of Contents

Introduction 1
Week of Ash Wednesday 3
   Ash Wednesday (Year A) 3
   Ash Wednesday (Year B) 5
   Ash Wednesday (Year C) 7
   Thursday after Ash Wednesday 8
   Friday after Ash Wednesday 10
   Saturday after Ash Wednesday 12

First Week of Lent 15
   First Sunday of Lent (Year A) 15
   First Sunday of Lent (Year B) 17
   First Sunday of Lent (Year C) 18
   Monday of the First Week of Lent 21
   Tuesday of the First Week of Lent 22
   Wednesday of the First Week of Lent 24
   Thursday of the First Week of Lent 26
   Friday of the First Week of Lent 27
   Saturday of the First Week of Lent 29

Second Week of Lent 31
   Second Sunday of Lent (Year A) 31
   Second Sunday of Lent (Year B) 33
   Second Sunday of Lent (Year C) 34
   Monday of the Second Week of Lent 36
   Tuesday of the Second Week of Lent 38
   Wednesday of the Second Week of Lent 40
   Thursday of the Second Week of Lent 41
   Friday of the Second Week of Lent 43
   Saturday of the Second Week of Lent 45

Third Week of Lent ... 47
- Third Sunday of Lent (Year A) ... 47
- Third Sunday of Lent (Year B) ... 49
- Third Sunday of Lent (Year C) ... 50
- Monday of the Third Week of Lent ... 52
- Tuesday of the Third Week of Lent ... 54
- Wednesday of the Third Week of Lent ... 55
- Thursday of the Third Week of Lent ... 57
- Friday of the Third Week of Lent ... 58
- Saturday of the Third Week of Lent ... 60

Fourth Week of Lent ... 63
- Fourth Sunday of Lent (Year A) ... 63
- Fourth Sunday of Lent (Year B) ... 65
- Fourth Sunday of Lent (Year C) ... 66
- Monday of the Fourth Week of Lent ... 68
- Tuesday of the Fourth Week of Lent ... 69
- Wednesday of the Fourth Week of Lent ... 71
- Thursday of the Fourth Week of Lent ... 72
- Friday of the Fourth Week of Lent ... 74
- Saturday of the Fourth Week of Lent ... 76

Fifth Week of Lent ... 79
- Fifth Sunday of Lent (Year A) ... 79
- Fifth Sunday of Lent (Year B) ... 81
- Fifth Sunday of Lent (Year C) ... 82
- Monday of the Fifth Week of Lent ... 84
- Tuesday of the Fifth Week of Lent ... 86
- Wednesday of the Fifth Week of Lent ... 87
- Thursday of the Fifth Week of Lent ... 89
- Friday of the Fifth Week of Lent ... 91
- Saturday of the Fifth Week of Lent ... 93

Holy Week 97
Palm Sunday of the Lord's Passion (Year A) 97
Palm Sunday of the Lord's Passion (Year B)....................... 99
Palm Sunday of the Lord's Passion (Year C) 101
Monday of Holy Week... 103
Tuesday of Holy Week... 105
Wednesday of Holy Week.. 106
Holy Thursday, Mass of the Lord's Supper (Reflection 1) 108
Holy Thursday, Mass of the Lord's Supper (Reflection 2) 110
Good Friday of the Lord's Passion (Reflection 1) 112
Good Friday of the Lord's Passion (Reflection 2) 115
Holy Saturday 118

Octave of Easter 121
Easter Sunday (Year A).. 121
Easter Sunday (Year B) 123
Easter Sunday (Year C) 125
Monday in the Octave of Easter.. 127
Tuesday in the Octave of Easter.. 129
Wednesday in the Octave of Easter 130
Thursday in the Octave of Easter...................................... 132
Friday in the Octave of Easter... 134
Saturday in the Octave of Easter 136
Divine Mercy Sunday (Year A) 138
Divine Mercy Sunday (Year B) 140
Divine Mercy Sunday (Year C) 143

Second Week of Easter 147
Monday of the Second Week of Easter............................. 147
Tuesday of the Second Week of Easter............................. 148
Wednesday of the Second Week of Easter........................ 149
Thursday of the Second Week of Easter........................... 151
Friday of the Second Week of Easter................................ 152
Saturday of the Second Week of Easter 154

Third Week of Easter 157
   Third Sunday of Easter (Years A) 157
   Third Sunday of Easter (Year B) 159
   Third Sunday of Easter (Year C) 161
   Monday of the Third Week of Easter................................. 163
   Tuesday of the Third Week of Easter 164
   Wednesday of the Third Week of Easter 166
   Thursday of the Third Week of Easter.............................. 167
   Friday of the Third Week of Easter.................................... 168
   Saturday of the Third Week of Easter................................ 170

Fourth Week of Easter..173
   Fourth Sunday of Easter (Year A)...................................... 173
   Fourth Sunday of Easter (Year B) 174
   Fourth Sunday of Easter (Year C) 176
   Monday of the Fourth Week of Easter 178
   Tuesday of the Fourth Week of Easter 179
   Wednesday of the Fourth Week of Easter 181
   Thursday of the Fourth Week of Easter 183
   Friday of the Fourth Week of Easter 184
   Saturday of the Fourth Week of Easter............................. 186

Fifth Week of Easter 189
   Fifth Sunday of Easter (Year A) 189
   Fifth Sunday of Easter (Year B) 190
   Fifth Sunday of Easter (Year C) 192
   Monday of the Fifth Week of Easter................................. 193
   Tuesday of the Fifth Week of Easter................................. 195
   Wednesday of the Fifth Week of Easter 196
   Thursday of the Fifth Week of Easter............................... 198
   Friday of the Fifth Week of Easter.................................... 199
   Saturday of the Fifth Week of Easter................................ 200

Sixth Week of Easter 203
  Sixth Sunday of Easter (Year A) 203
  Sixth Sunday of Easter (Year B) 204
  Sixth Sunday of Easter (Year C) 206
  Monday of the Sixth Week of Easter 207
  Tuesday of the Sixth Week of Easter 209
  Wednesday of the Sixth Week of Easter 210
  Thursday of the Sixth Week of Easter,
    (When the Ascension is transferred to Sunday) 211
  Solemnity of the Ascension of the Lord 213
  Friday of the Sixth Week of Easter..................................... 214
  Saturday of the Sixth Week of Easter................................. 216

Seventh Week of Easter..219
  Seventh Sunday of Easter,
    (When the Ascension was celebrated Thursday)............. 219
  Monday of the Seventh Week of Easter............................. 220
  Tuesday of the Seventh Week of Easter............................. 222
  Wednesday of the Seventh Week of Easter........................ 223
  Thursday of the Seventh Week of Easter........................... 225
  Friday of the Seventh Week of Easter................................ 226
  Saturday of the Seventh Week of Easter 228

Feasts and Solemnities 231
  Feast of the Chair of St. Peter, February 22 231
  Solemnity of Saint Joseph, Husband of Mary, March 19.. 233
  Solemnity of the Annunciation, March 25 235
  Feast of Saint Mark, April 25.. 237
  Feast of Saints Philip and James, Apostles, May 3 238
  Feast of Saint Matthias, Apostle, May 14 240
  Feast of Visitation of the Blessed Virgin Mary, May 31.... 242
  Solemnity of Pentecost Sunday... 243
  Memorial of the Blessed Virgin Mary,
    Mother of the Church—Monday after Pentecost........... 246

Additional Books in This Series...249

Introduction

Lent is one of the best times of the year for spiritual renewal. In some ways, it can be considered a forty-day retreat lived each year within the context of your daily life. Most Catholics have understood the importance of Lent since childhood on account of Lenten practices, such as being marked with ashes, abstaining from meat on Fridays and giving something up as a sacrifice. All of these practices help to bear spiritual fruit in our lives.

One of the most important parts of our Lenten practice is that of engaging the Holy Scriptures in a powerful and personal way. Scripture is the Word of God. Therefore, with the Word of God, we encounter Jesus Himself as we prayerfully reflect upon it. Reading and meditating on the Scriptures is a way of allowing our Divine Lord to speak to us, draw us to Himself and communicate His perfect and all-consuming love.

The goal of this *Catholic Daily Reflections Series* is to help the reader to meet our Lord personally during the Lenten and Easter season. Jesus' love for each of us is intense and potentially transforming in every way, if we are willing to allow Him into our lives.

Lent is a time through which we more directly look at the sacrificial love of God. We ponder the Sacrifice of the Cross and all that Jesus suffered so as to set us free. By looking at the Cross more directly each Lent, we discover just how far God is willing to go to enter into a relationship of love with each one of us. He held nothing back and did not even spare His own life. We must learn to open ourselves up fully to this love, and Lent is the ideal time to do so.

Though the central focus of Lent is the Cross, the end of the story is the Resurrection. We know that our Divine Lord conquered sin and death through His suffering and rose victorious on the third day. Thus, the Cross must always be seen in the light of this final victory and must allow us to be filled with hope as we walk through our own suffering in life.

Commit yourself to a daily reading of the Sacred Scripture this Lent and Easter and, to the extent that this book assists you with that, allow our Lord to change your life. He is the Living Word, and He desires to become more fully the Lord of your life!

How to Use this Book

This book is formatted in such a way that it can be used year after year. It is not dated for one particular year but covers every Gospel option within the Lectionary. For that reason, some of the reflections will not be used during each calendar year.

The Table of Contents offers a quick and detailed description of each reflection so that you can quickly and easily find the correct reflection for the day.

If you need assistance in determining the liturgical celebration for the day, you can view or print our online calendar at:

www.mycatholic.life/calendar

Or you can visit the liturgical calendar of the United States Bishops Conference at: www.usccb.org

Week of Ash Wednesday

Pray, Fast, Give

Ash Wednesday (Year A)

> "And your Father who sees in secret will repay you."
> Matthew 6:4b

Lent begins. 40 days to pray, fast and grow in charity. We need this time each year to step back and reexamine our lives, to turn away from our sins and to grow in the virtues God so deeply desires to bestow upon us. The 40 days of Lent are to be an imitation of Jesus' 40 days in the desert. In fact, we are called not only to "imitate" Jesus' time in the desert, we are called to live this time with Him, in Him and through Him.

Jesus did not personally need to spend 40 days of fasting and prayer in the desert so as to obtain a deeper holiness. He is Holiness Itself! He is the Holy One of God. He is Perfection. He is the Second Person of the Most Holy Trinity. He is God. But Jesus entered into the desert to fast and pray so as to invite us to join Him and to receive the transforming qualities He manifested in His human nature as He endured the suffering of those 40 days. Are you ready for your 40 days in the desert with our Lord?

While in the desert, Jesus manifested every perfection within His human nature. And although no one saw this but the Father in Heaven, His time in the desert was abundantly fruitful for the human race. It was abundantly fruitful for each one of us.

The "desert" we are called to enter is one that is hidden from the eyes of those around us but is visible to the Father in Heaven. It's "hidden" in that our growth in virtue is not done for vainglory, for selfish recognition, or to obtain worldly praise. The 40 day desert we must enter is one that transforms us by drawing us to deeper prayer, detachment from anything not of God, and fills us with love of those we encounter every day.

During these 40 days, we must pray. Properly speaking, prayer means we communicate with God on an interior level. We do more than attend Mass or speak prayers aloud. Prayer is first and foremost a secret and interior *communication* with God. We speak, but more than that, we listen, hear, understand and respond. Without all four of these qualities, prayer is not prayer. It's not "communication." It's only us talking to ourselves.

During these 40 days, we must fast. Especially in our day and age, our five senses are overwhelmed with activity and noise. Our eyes and ears are often dazzled by TV, radio, computers, etc. Our taste buds are constantly satiated with fine foods, sweets and comfort foods, often to excess. Our five senses need a break from the bombardment of the delights of the world so as to turn to the deeper delights of a life of union with God.

During these 40 days, we must give. Greed often takes hold of us without us even realizing the extent of its grip. We want this and that. We consume more and more material things. And we do so because we seek satisfaction from the world. We need to detach from all that distracts us from God, and generosity is one of the best ways to achieve this detachment.

Reflect, today, upon these three simple words: pray, fast and give. Seek to live these qualities in a hidden way known only to God this Lent. If you do so, the Lord will begin to do greater wonders in your life than you may currently realize are possible. He will free you from the selfishness that often binds us and will enable you to love Him and others on a whole new level.

My penitential Lord, I give myself to You this Lent. I freely choose to enter into the desert of these 40 days and choose to pray, fast and give of myself to an extent I have never done before. I pray that this Lent will be a time in which I am transformed interiorly by You. Set me free, dear Lord, from all that keeps me from loving You and others with all my heart. Jesus, I trust in You.

Lent—A Time for True Prayer

Ash Wednesday (Year B)

> But when you pray, go to your inner room, close the door, and pray to your Father in secret. And your Father who sees in secret will repay you. Matthew 6:6

One of the most important parts of true prayer is that it takes place deep in the inner room of your soul. It is there in the inner depths of your being that you will meet God. Saint Teresa of Ávila, one of the greatest spiritual writers in the history of our Church, describes the soul as a castle in which God dwells. Meeting Him, praying to Him and communing with Him requires that we enter into the deepest and innermost chamber within this castle of our soul. It is there, in the innermost dwelling, that the full glory and beauty of God is discovered.

God is not just a God who is "out there" far away in Heaven. He is a God Who is closer and more intimate than we could ever imagine. Lent is a time, more than any other time of the year, when we must strive to make that journey inward so as to discover the Indwelling of the Most Holy Trinity.

What does God want of you this Lent? It's easy to begin Lent with more superficial commitments, such as giving up a favorite food or doing an extra good deed. Some choose to use Lent as a time to get in better physical shape, and others decide to dedicate more time to spiritual reading or other holy exercises. All of this is good and useful. But you can be certain that the deepest desire of our Lord for you this Lent is that you pray.

Prayer, of course, is much more than saying prayers. It's not only saying the rosary, or meditating upon Scripture, or reciting beautifully composed prayers. Prayer is ultimately a relationship with God. It's an encounter with the Triune God Who dwells within you. True prayer is an act of love between you and your Beloved. It's an exchange of persons: your life for God's. Prayer is an act of union and communion by which we become one with God and God becomes one with us.

The great mystics have taught us that there are many levels to prayer. We often begin with the recitation of prayers, such as the beautiful prayer of the rosary. From there we meditate, ponder and reflect deeply upon the mysteries of our Lord and His life. We come to know Him more fully and, little by little, discover that we are no longer just thinking about God, but we are gazing at Him face to face.

As we begin the holy season of Lent, reflect upon your practice of prayer. If the images of prayer presented here intrigue you, then make a commitment to discover more. Commit yourself to the discovery of God in prayer. There is no limit and no end to the depth to which God wants to draw you through prayer. True prayer is never boring. When you discover true prayer, you discover the infinite mystery of God. And this discovery is more glorious than anything you could ever imagine in life.

My divine Lord, I give myself to You this Lent. Draw me in so that I may come to know You more. Reveal to me Your divine presence, dwelling deep within me, calling me to Yourself. May this Lent, dear Lord, be glorious as I strengthen my love and devotion through the discovery of the gift of true prayer. Jesus, I trust in You.

Being Set Free for Love

Ash Wednesday (Year C)

> Be merciful, O Lord, for we have sinned. (see Psalm 51)

Mercy. That's what it's all about. As we begin Lent, a great place to start is with a better understanding of mercy.

Often when we think about Lent, we think of it with a sort of dread. "I have to give something up," we often think. But if that is our thought, then we are missing the point. Do I "have to" give something up? Well, yes and no. It's true that God wills this and has spoken this practice of self-denial and self-discipline to us through His Church. That is true. But it's much more of an invitation to grace than the imposition of a burden.

Giving something up is really all about entering into God's abundant mercy on a deeper level. It's about being freed from all that binds us, and it helps us experience the new life we so deeply seek. Giving something up could refer to something as simple as fasting from a food or drink. Or, it can be any intentional act that requires a certain self-denial. But this is good! Why? Because it strengthens us in our spirit and our will. It strengthens us to be more resolved to say "Yes" to God on that complete level.

So often in life we are controlled by our emotions and desires. We have an impulse for this or that or to do this or that, and we often let those impulses or desires control us. Entering into a practice of self-denial helps strengthen us to control our disordered tendencies rather than being controlled by them. And this applies to much more than just food and drink. It applies to many things in life including our life of virtue, especially our charity.

Mercy is all about charity. It's about love in the way God wants us to love. It's about being free to let love consume us and take us over so that, in the end, all we want to do is love. This can be a hard practice to establish in our lives but is the source of our joy and fulfillment.

Mercy, in particular, is an act of love that, in a sense, is not deserved by another. It's a free gift that is given purely from the motivation of love. And this is exactly the love God gives us. God's love is all mercy. And if we want to receive that mercy, then we also have to give it. And if we want to give it, we need to properly dispose ourselves to giving mercy. This is accomplished, in part, by our little acts of self-denial.

So make this a great Lent, but don't get stuck thinking that the Lenten sacrifices are burdensome. They are one essential piece of the pathway to the life God wants to bestow upon us.

My sacrificial Lord, may this Lent be truly fruitful in my life. May it be a grace and a joy to embrace all that You wish to bestow upon me. Jesus, I do trust in You.

The World or Your Soul?

Thursday after Ash Wednesday

> "What profit is there for one to gain the whole world yet lose or forfeit himself?" Luke 9:25

Many people dream of winning the lottery. And oftentimes, the dream is for many millions of dollars. Imagine what you would do if you became an instant millionaire or an instant billionaire. Do you find yourself daydreaming about this?

If so, perhaps the question above is a good one to ponder. What good is it if you win the biggest lottery in history, become the wealthiest person on the face of the Earth, but lack the grace of God in your life and lack faith? Would you trade your faith for being exceptionally wealthy and gaining the whole world? Many people probably would or else Jesus would not have asked this question.

Very often in life we have the wrong priorities. We seek instant satisfaction and gratification over eternal fulfillment. It's hard for many people to live with an eternal perspective.

Some may say, "Well, I choose both! I want the whole world and the salvation of my soul!" But Jesus' question presupposes that we cannot have both. We must pick which one we choose to pursue. Choosing a life of faith and the salvation of our souls requires that we let go of many things in this world. Even if God were to bless us with much in this world, we must strive to live in such a way that we are ready and willing to "give it up" if it were beneficial to our eternal salvation, or the salvation of others. This is hard to do and requires a very deep love of God. It requires that we are convinced, on the deepest level, that the pursuit of holiness is more important than anything else.

Reflect, today, upon this profound question from Jesus. Know that He poses it to you. How do you respond? Do not hesitate to make God and His abundant mercy the central focus of your life. Lent is one of the best times of the year to seriously look at the most fundamental desire and goal of your heart. Choose Him above all else and you will be eternally grateful you did.

My eternal Lord, as we enter into this Lenten season, give me the grace I need to look at my priorities. Help me to honestly discern that which is the most fundamental and central driving motivation of my life. Help me to choose You above all else so that You will help everything in my life to become ordered in accord with Your holy will. Jesus, I trust in You.

A Day to Fast and Abstain

Friday after Ash Wednesday

> "The days will come when the bridegroom is taken away from them, and then they will fast." Matthew 9:15

Fridays in Lent…are you ready for them? Every Friday in Lent is a day of abstinence from meat. So be sure to embrace this little sacrifice today in union with our entire Church. What a blessing it is to offer sacrifice as an entire Church!

Fridays in Lent (and, in fact, throughout the year) are also days in which the Church asks us to do some form of penance. Abstinence from meat certainly falls into that category, unless you dislike meat and love fish. The most important thing to understand about Fridays in Lent is that they should be a day of sacrifice. Jesus offered the ultimate sacrifice on a Friday and endured the most excruciating pain for the atonement of our sins. We should not hesitate to offer our own sacrifice and to strive to spiritually unite that sacrifice to Christ's. Why would we do that?

At the heart of the answer to that question is a basic understanding of redemption from sin. It's important to understand the unique and profound teaching of our Catholic Church on this. As Catholics, we do share a common belief with other Christians throughout the world that Jesus is the one and only Savior of the world. The only way to Heaven is through the redemption won by His Cross. In a sense, Jesus "paid the price" of death for our sins. He took on our punishment.

But with that said, we must understand our role and responsibility in receiving this priceless gift. It's not simply a gift that God offers by saying, "OK, I paid the price, now you're completely off the hook." No, we believe He says something more like this, "I have opened the door to salvation through my suffering and death. Now I invite you to enter that door with me and unite your own sufferings with mine so that my sufferings, united with yours, will bring you to salvation and freedom from sin." So, in a sense, we are not "off the hook;" rather, we now have a way to freedom and salvation by uniting our lives, sufferings and sins to the Cross of Christ. As Catholics, we understand that salvation came at a price and that the price was not only the death of Jesus, it's also our willing participation in His suffering and death. This is the way that His Sacrifice transforms our particular sins.

Fridays in Lent are days in which we are especially invited to unite ourselves, voluntarily and freely, with the Sacrifice of Jesus. His Sacrifice required of Him great selflessness and self-denial. The small acts of fasting, abstinence and other forms of self-denial you choose dispose your will to be more conformed to Christ's so as to be able to more completely unite yourself with Him, receiving the grace of salvation.

Reflect, today, upon the small sacrifices you are called to make this Lent—especially on Fridays in Lent. Make the choice to be sacrificial today and you will discover that it is the best way to enter into a deeper union with the Savior of the World.

Most sacrificial Lord, I choose, this day, to become one with You in Your suffering and death. I offer You my suffering and my sin. Please forgive my sin and allow my suffering, especially that which results from my sin, to be transformed by Your own suffering so that I can share in the joy of Your Resurrection. May the small sacrifices and acts of self-denial I offer You become a source of my deeper union with You. Jesus, I trust in You.

The Divine Physician "Needs" the Sick

Saturday after Ash Wednesday

> "Those who are healthy do not need a physician, but the sick do. I have not come to call the righteous to repentance but sinners." Luke 5:31–32

What would a doctor do without patients? What if no one were sick? The poor doctor would be out of business. Therefore, in a sense, it's fair to say that a doctor *needs* the sick in order to fulfill his role.

The same could be said of Jesus. He is the Savior of the World. But what if there were no sinners? Then Jesus' death would have been in vain, and His mercy would not be necessary. Therefore, in a sense, we can conclude that Jesus, as the Savior of the World, *needs* sinners. He needs those who have turned away from Him, violated the Divine Law, violated their own dignity, violated the dignity of others and acted in a selfish and sinful way. Jesus needs sinners. Why? Because Jesus is the Savior, and a Savior needs to save. A Savior needs those who need to be saved in order to save!

This is important to understand, because when we do, we will suddenly realize that coming to Jesus, with the filth of our sin, brings great joy to His Heart. It brings joy, because He is able to fulfill the mission given Him by the Father, exercising His mercy as the one and only Savior.

Allow Jesus to fulfill His mission! Let Him offer mercy to you! You do this by admitting your need for mercy. You do this by coming to Him in a vulnerable and sinful state, unworthy of mercy and worthy only of eternal damnation. Coming to Jesus in this way allows Him to fulfill the mission given Him by the Father. It allows Him to manifest, in a concrete way, His Heart of abundant mercy. Jesus "needs" you to fulfill His mission. Give Him this gift and let Him be your merciful Savior.

Reflect, today, upon the mercy of God from a new perspective. Look at it from the perspective of Jesus as the Divine Physician who desires to fulfill His healing mission. Realize that He needs you in order to fulfill His mission. He needs you to admit your sin and be open to His healing. In so doing, you allow the gates of mercy to pour forth in abundance in our day and age.

Dear Savior and Divine Physician, I thank You for coming to save and heal. I thank You for Your burning desire to manifest Your mercy in my life. Please humble me so that I may be open to Your healing touch and that, through this gift of salvation, I allow You to manifest Your Divine Mercy. Jesus, I trust in You.

First Week of Lent

Facing Temptation

First Sunday of Lent (Year A)

> Then Jesus was led by the Spirit into the desert to be tempted by the devil. He fasted for forty days and forty nights, and afterwards he was hungry. Matthew 4:1–2

Is temptation good? Certainly it's not a sin to be tempted. Otherwise our Lord could never have been tempted Himself. But He was. And so are we. As we enter into the first full week of Lent, we are given the opportunity to ponder the story of Jesus' temptation in the desert.

Temptation is never from God. But God does permit us to be tempted. Not so that we fall, but so that we grow in holiness. Temptation forces us to rise up and make a choice either for God or for the temptation. Though mercy and forgiveness are always offered when we fail, the blessings that await those who overcome temptation are numerous.

Jesus' temptation did not increase His holiness, but it did afford Him the opportunity to manifest His perfection within His human nature. It is that perfection we seek and His perfection that we must strive to imitate as we face the temptations of life. Let's look at five clear "blessings" that can come from enduring the temptations of the evil one. Ponder these carefully and slowly:

> First, enduring a temptation and conquering it helps us see the strength of God in our lives.

> Second, temptation humbles us, stripping away our pride and our struggle of thinking we are self-reliant and self-made.

> Third, there is great value in completely rejecting the devil. This not only robs him of his ongoing power to

deceive us, but it also clarifies our vision of who he is so that we can continue to reject him and his works.

Fourth, overcoming temptation clearly and definitively strengthens us in every virtue.

Fifth, the devil would not tempt us if he were not concerned about our holiness. Thus, we should see temptation as a sign that the evil one is losing hold of our lives.

Overcoming temptation is like acing an exam, winning a contest, completing a difficult project or accomplishing some challenging feat. We should take great joy in overcoming temptation in our lives, realizing that this strengthens us to the core of our being. As we do so, we must also do so in humility, realizing that we have not accomplished this on our own but only by the grace of God in our lives.

The opposite is true also. When we fail a particular temptation over and over again, we get discouraged and tend to lose the little virtue we have. Know that any and every temptation from the evil one <u>can</u> be overcome. Nothing is too great. Nothing is too difficult. Humble yourself in confession, seek the help of a confidant, fall on your knees in prayer, trust in the almighty power of God. Overcoming temptation is not only possible, it is a glorious and transforming experience of grace in your life.

Reflect, today, upon Jesus facing the devil in the desert after spending 40 days of fasting. He faced every temptation of the evil one so as to assure us that if we but unite ourselves completely to Him in His human nature, so we also will have His strength to overcome anything and everything the vile devil throws our way.

My dear Lord, after spending 40 days of fasting and prayer in the dry and hot desert, You allowed Yourself to be tempted by the evil one.

The devil attacked You with all he had, and You easily, quickly and definitively defeated him, rejecting his lies and deceptions. Give me the grace I need to overcome every temptation I encounter and to rely completely upon You without reserve. Jesus, I trust in You.

40 Days in the Desert

First Sunday of Lent (Year B)

> The Spirit drove Jesus out into the desert, and he remained in the desert for forty days, tempted by Satan. He was among wild beasts, and the angels ministered to him. Mark 1:12–13

Today's Gospel from Mark presents us with a short version of the Temptation of Jesus in the desert. Matthew and Luke give many more details, such as Jesus' threefold temptation from satan. But Mark simply states the fact that Jesus was driven into the desert for forty days and was tempted.

What's interesting to note is that it was "The Spirit" Who drove Jesus into the desert. Jesus did not go there against His will; He went there freely in accord with the will of the Father and by the direction of the Holy Spirit. Why would the Spirit drive Jesus into the desert for this time of fasting, prayer and temptation?

First of all, this time of temptation took place immediately after Jesus was baptized by John. And though Jesus Himself did not spiritually need that baptism, these two series of events teach us much. The truth is that when we choose to follow Christ and live out our baptism, we receive a new strength to fight evil. The grace is there. As a new creation in Christ, you have all the grace you need to conquer the evil one, sin and temptation. Jesus, therefore, set for us an example in order to teach us this truth. He was baptized and then was driven into the desert to face the evil one so as to tell us that we also can conquer him and his evil lies.

As Jesus was in the desert enduring these temptations, "the angels ministered to him." The same is true with us. Our Lord does not leave us alone in the midst of our daily temptations. Rather, He always sends us His angels to minister to us and to help us defeat this vile enemy.

What is your greatest temptation in life? Perhaps you struggle with a habit of sin that you fail at time and time again. Perhaps it's a temptation of the flesh, or a struggle with anger, self-righteousness, dishonesty or something else. Whatever your temptation may be, know that you have all you need to overcome it on account of the grace given to you by your Baptism, strengthened by your Confirmation and regularly fed by your participation in the Most Holy Eucharist.

Reflect, today, upon whatever your temptations may be. See the Person of Christ facing those temptations with you and in you. Know that His strength is given to you if you but trust Him with unwavering confidence.

My tempted Lord, You allowed Yourself to endure the humiliation of being tempted by satan himself. You did so to show me and all Your children that we can overcome our own temptations through You and by Your strength. Help me, dear Lord, to daily turn to You with my struggles so that You will be victorious in me. Jesus, I trust in You.

Temptation is Real, and Painful

First Sunday of Lent (Year C)

> Filled with the Holy Spirit, Jesus returned from the Jordan and was led by the Spirit into the desert for forty days, to be tempted by the devil. Luke 4:1–2a

What a painful experience for Jesus. If you really think about this, it can be difficult to understand...at least at first.

Jesus, the Son of God, the Messiah, the Creator of the Universe, the great I AM, the second Person of the Most Holy Trinity, is in the desert, suffering for forty days while He is tempted by the devil and living among the wild beasts. Why in the world would He do this and why would God the Father allow it to happen? And what's more, it says that it was actually the Holy Spirit who drove Jesus into the desert to experience this painful 40 days!

Perhaps we rarely reflect upon all that Jesus endured and all that He suffered in His human life. Sure, we think about the Crucifixion at times, but even that is often overshadowed by our knowledge that He rose. It's easy to miss the suffering He experienced throughout His life. And it's easy to miss the reason He went through all that He did go through in His humanity.

So what's it all about? It's about love for us all. It's about God loving us so much that He was willing to endure every form of hardship and human suffering that enters into our lives. It's about God being able to look us square in the face and say, "Yes, I do understand what you're going through…I really do." This is love. It's a love so deep that God Himself was willing to experience our weaknesses and pain so that He would be able to meet us there, console us in the midst of whatever we are going through, and gently lift us out of it to the new life He has in store for us. Again, this is Love!

The Spirit "led" (Matthew's and Luke's versions) and even "drove" (Mark's version) Jesus out into the desert. This was a way of telling us that this experience was the plan and will of God. It wasn't something imposed upon Jesus by some strange happenstance. It wasn't bad luck or an unfortunate and meaningless human suffering. No, it was suffering for a purpose. Suffering with an intention. And the intention was, in part, to experience and embrace all that we experience and must embrace.

Temptation in life is real. It's the result of our fallen human nature. It comes from our weakness but also from the evil one. Temptation can be a heavy burden and cause heavy emotional and psychological pain. And when the temptation is given in to, it causes an even deeper spiritual pain. Jesus never gave in to the temptations in the desert, nor did He give in to temptations at any other time in His life. But He endured them and suffered them.

This tells us that He can be our strength and inspiration in the midst of whatever we are tempted with each and every day. Some days we may feel the loneliness and isolation of one who is driven into the desert of our sins. We may feel as though the wild beasts of our disordered passions are getting the best of us. We may feel as though the evil one is having his way with us. Well, Jesus felt this way, also. And He freely allowed Himself to experience this in His humanity. It was the will of the Father and the working of the Holy Spirit that drove Him to this experience.

For these reasons, it is Jesus Himself who is able to meet you in this desert within. He is there, waiting for you, looking for you, calling to you. He is there in the midst of anything and everything you may be going through. And it is He, the One who defeated this desert temptation, who will gently guide you out. He went to the desert to meet you and to bring you back. And just as the angels ministered to Jesus in this desert, so also does He send those angels to minister to you.

So whether your "desert" is only a slight agitation in life right now, or if it's a struggle against complete despair, Jesus wants to meet you and bring you out. He conquered the desert once and for all, and He is able to conquer any desert in your life, also.

Lord, I acknowledge Your perfect love for me. I believe that You love me enough to endure all suffering, to understand all suffering, and to bring me out of my own interior dryness and pain. May I let you be driven into the desert of my own soul; and there, as I encounter You, may I allow You to lead me to the cool and refreshing waters. Jesus, I trust in You.

Serving Christ in Others

Monday of the First Week of Lent

> "Amen, I say to you, whatever you did for one of these least brothers of mine, you did for me." Matthew 25:40

Who is that "least brother?" It's interesting that Jesus specifically points to the person considered the least, as opposed to a more general statement that includes all people. Why not say, "Whatever you do to others…?" This would include all whom we serve. But instead Jesus pointed to the least brother. Perhaps this should be seen, especially, as the most sinful person, the weakest, the most gravely ill, the incapacitated, the hungry and the homeless, and all those who have pronounced needs in this life.

The most beautiful and touching part about this statement is that Jesus *identifies* Himself with the person in need, the "least" of all. By serving those in special need, we are serving Jesus. But for Him to be able to say that, He has to be intimately united with these people. And by showing such an intimate connection to them, Jesus reveals their infinite dignity as persons.

This is such an important point to grasp! In fact, this has been a central theme in the constant teachings of St. John Paul II, Pope Benedict XVI, and Pope Francis. An invitation to constant focus upon the dignity and value of the person must be the central message we take from this passage.

Reflect, today, upon the dignity of each and every person. Try to call to mind anyone you may fail to look at with perfect respect. Who is it you look down upon and roll your eyes at? Who is it you judge or disdain? It is within this person, more than any other, that Jesus waits for you. He waits to meet you and to have you love Him in the weak and the sinner. Reflect upon their dignity. Identify the person who fits this description the most in your life and commit yourself to love and serve them. For in them you will love and serve our Lord.

Dear Lord, I do understand and believe that You are present, in hidden form, in the weakest of the weak, the poorest of the poor and in the sinner in our midst. Help me to diligently seek You out in each and every person I encounter, especially those in most need. As I find You, may I love You and serve You with my whole heart. Jesus, I trust in You.

Forgiving Others and Being Forgiven

Tuesday of the First Week of Lent

"If you forgive men their transgressions, your heavenly Father will forgive you. But if you do not forgive men, neither will your Father forgive your transgressions." Matthew 6:14–15

This passage presents us with an ideal we must strive for. It also presents us with the consequences if we do not strive for this ideal. Forgive and be forgiven. Both must be desired and sought after.

When forgiveness is properly understood, it is much easier to desire, give and receive. When it is not properly understood, forgiveness can be seen as a confusing and heavy burden and, therefore, as something undesirable.

Perhaps the greatest challenge to the act of forgiving another is the sense of "justice" that can appear to be lost when forgiveness is given. This is especially true when forgiveness is offered to someone who fails to ask forgiveness. On the contrary, when one does ask for forgiveness, and expresses true remorse, it is much easier to forgive and to abandon the feeling that the offender should "pay" for what was done. But when there is a lack of sorrow on the part of the offender, this leaves what can feel like a lack of justice if forgiveness is offered. This can be a difficult feeling to overcome by ourselves.

It's important to note that forgiving another does not excuse their sin. Forgiveness does not mean that the sin did not happen or that it is OK that it happened. Rather, forgiving another does the opposite. Forgiving actually points to the sin, acknowledges it and makes it a central focus. This is important to understand. By identifying the sin that is to be forgiven, and then forgiving it, justice is done in a supernatural way. Justice is fulfilled by mercy. And the mercy offered has an even greater effect on the one offering mercy than the one it is offered to.

By offering mercy for the sin of another, we become freed of the effects of their sin. Mercy is a way for God to remove this hurt from our lives and free us to encounter His mercy all the more by the forgiveness of our own sins for which we could never deserve on our own effort.

It's also important to note that forgiving another does not necessarily result in reconciliation. *Reconciliation* between the two can only happen when the offender accepts the forgiveness offered after humbly admitting their sin. This humble and purifying act satisfies justice on a whole new level and enables these sins to be transformed into grace. And once transformed, they can even go so far as to deepen the bond of love between the two.

Reflect, today, upon the person you most need to forgive. Who is it and what have they done that has offended you? Do not be afraid to offer the mercy of forgiveness and do not hesitate in doing so. The mercy you offer will bring forth the justice of God in a way that you could never accomplish by your own efforts. This act of forgiving also frees you from the burden of that sin, and enables God to forgive you of your sins.

My forgiving Lord, I am a sinner who is in need of Your mercy. Help me to have a heart of true sorrow for my sins and to turn to You for that grace. As I seek Your mercy, help me to also forgive the sins that others have committed against me. I do forgive. Help that forgiveness to enter deep into my whole being as an expression of Your holy and Divine Mercy. Jesus, I trust in You.

Responding to the Call to Repent
Wednesday of the First Week of Lent

"At the judgment the men of Nineveh will arise with this generation and condemn it, because at the preaching of Jonah they repented, and there is something greater than Jonah here." Luke 11:32

What an interesting way for Jesus to call the people to repentance. Simply put, the people of Nineveh repented when Jonah preached to them. However, the people in Jesus' time did not. The result is that, at the end of time, the people of Nineveh will be given the responsibility of condemning those who failed to listen to Jesus.

The first thing we should take from this is that condemnation for refusing to repent of one's sins is real and serious. Jesus is speaking about eternal damnation to the people who fail to listen to His preaching. As a result of this very strong teaching of Jesus, we should sincerely look at our own willingness to repent, or lack thereof.

Secondly, it's important to point out that the people Jesus chastised were far more blessed with the prophetic message than the people of Jonah's time. Remember that Jonah was a man who, at first, ran from God and from his mission. He did not want to go to Nineveh and only did so after being brought there in the belly of a whale against his will. It's hard to imagine that Jonah would have subsequently preached with a wholehearted zeal. But, nonetheless, his preaching was effective.

The people of Jesus' time were blessed with hearing the actual words of the Savior of the World. But so are we! We have the Gospels, the teachings of the Church, the witness of the great saints, the shepherding of the Holy Father, the Sacraments and so much more. We have countless methods of obtaining the Gospel message in our technological age and, yet, we can easily fail to heed Christ's message.

Reflect, today, upon your own willing response to the words of Jesus. He speaks to us in powerful ways and yet we so often fail to listen. Our failure to listen leads to a failure of complete repentance from our sins. If this is you, reflect also upon the words of severe condemnation that await those who are obstinate. This realization should fill us with a holy fear and motivate us to listen to the preaching of our Lord.

Savior of the World, I know You speak to me in countless ways. You preach through Your Scriptures, Your Church and in my life of prayer. Help me to heed Your voice and accept all You say with perfect obedience and submission. I love You, my dear Lord, and I repent of my sin. Jesus, I trust in You.

Ask, and All Good Things Will Be Given You

Thursday of the First Week of Lent

> "Ask and it will be given to you; seek and you will find; knock and the door will be opened to you…"
>
> "How much more will your heavenly Father give good things to those who ask him." Matthew 7:7, 11

Jesus is very clear that when we ask, we will receive, when we seek, we will find, and when we knock, the door will be opened to you. But is that your experience? Sometimes we can ask, and ask, and beg, and it appears that our prayer goes unanswered, at least in the way we want it to be answered. So what does Jesus mean when He says to "ask…seek…knock" and you will receive?

The key to understanding this exhortation from our Lord is that, as the Scripture above states, through our prayer, God will give "<u>good things</u> to those who ask." He doesn't promise us whatever we ask for; rather, He promises that which is truly good and good, in particular, for our eternal salvation.

This begs the question, "Then how do I pray and what do I pray for?" Ideally, every prayer of intercession we utter should be for the Lord's will to be done, nothing more, and nothing less. Only His perfect will.

That can be harder to pray for than one might first expect. Too often we tend to pray that "<u>my</u> will be done" rather than that "<u>Thy</u> will be done." But if we can trust, and trust on a profound level, that God's will is perfect and provides us with all "good things," then seeking His will, asking for it and knocking at the door of His heart will produce an abundance of grace as God desires to bestow it.

Reflect, today, upon the way you pray. Try to change your prayer so that it seeks the good things God wants to bestow rather than the many things you want God to bestow. It may be hard at first to detach from your own ideas and your own will, but in the end, you will be blessed with many good things from God.

Lord of true goodness, I do pray that Your will be done in all things. I desire to surrender to You above all, and to trust in Your perfect plan. Help me, dear Lord, to abandon my own ideas and desires, and to seek Your will always. Jesus, I trust in You.

Being Real, Being Honest, Being Sincere

Friday of the First Week of Lent

> "I tell you, unless your righteousness surpasses that of the scribes and Pharisees, you will not enter into the Kingdom of heaven." Matthew 5:20

Who wants to enter the Kingdom of Heaven? Certainly all of us do! That should be our primary goal in life. And, along with that goal, we should seek to bring as many people with us as possible.

Too often we fail to see this as an ultimate goal in life. We fail to keep our eyes on Heaven as the primary reason we are here on Earth. It's very easy to get caught up in the day-to-day satisfactions of what we may call the "mini goals" of life. These are goals such as entertainment, money, success, and the like. And we can often make these mini goals our *only* goals at times.

So how about you? What is your goal? What is it you strive for and seek throughout your day? If you honestly examine your actions throughout each day you may be surprised that you are actually seeking unimportant and passing mini goals more than you realize.

Jesus gives us one bit of clear direction in this passage above on how to attain that ultimate goal of life—the Kingdom of Heaven. The path He points to is *righteousness*.

What is righteousness? It's simply being real. Being authentic. Not fake. And most especially, it's being real in our love of God. The Pharisees struggled with pretending they were holy and good followers of the will of God. But they were not very good at it. They may have been good at the acting job, and they may have convinced themselves and others, but they could not fool Jesus. Jesus could see through the fake veneer and perceive that which was underneath. He could see that their "righteousness" was only a show for themselves and others.

Reflect, today, upon your own righteousness—your honesty and sincerity in striving for holiness. If you want to daily keep Heaven as your ultimate goal, then you must also strive to make each daily mini goal an honest attempt at holiness. We must daily seek Christ with all sincerity and truth in all the small things of life. We must then let that sincerity shine through, showing what truly lies beneath. To be righteous, in the truest sense, means we sincerely seek God throughout our day and make that sincerity the constant goal of our life.

Lord of true righteousness, make me righteous. Please help me to be sincere in all that I do and all that I seek in life. Help me to love You and to love You each and every moment of the day. Jesus, I trust in You.

The Call to Perfection

Saturday of the First Week of Lent

> "So be perfect, just as your heavenly Father is perfect."
> Matthew 5:48

Perfection is our calling, nothing less. The danger in trying to shoot for something less is that you might actually attain it. Then what? In other words, if you settle only for being "pretty good" you might actually become "pretty good." But pretty good is not good enough according to Jesus. He wants perfection! This is a high calling.

What is perfection? It can seem overwhelming and almost beyond reasonable expectations. We may even get discouraged at the idea. But if we understand what perfection really is, then we may not be intimidated by the thought at all. In fact, we may find ourselves deeply desiring it and making it our new goal in life.

At first, perfection can seem like something only the great saints of old lived. But for every saint we may read about in a book, there are thousands more that have never been recorded in history and many other future saints living today. Imagine that. When we get to Heaven we will certainly be in awe of the great saints we know about. But think about the countless others that we will be introduced to for the first time in Heaven. These men and women strove for and found the path of true happiness. They discovered they were meant for perfection.

Perfection means we are striving to live each and every moment in the grace of God. That's all! Just living here and now immersed in God's grace. We do not yet have tomorrow, and yesterday is gone forever. All we have is this single present moment. And it's this moment that we are called to live perfectly.

Certainly each one of us can seek perfection for a moment. We can surrender to God here and now and seek only His will in this moment. We can pray, offer selfless charity, make an act of extraordinary kindness and the like. And if we can do it in this present moment then what's keeping us from doing it in the next moment?

Over time, the more we live each moment in God's grace and strive to surrender each moment over to His will, we get stronger, and we get holier. We slowly build habits that make each and every moment easier. Over time, the habits we form make us who we are and draw us into perfection.

Reflect, today, upon the present moment. Try not to think about the future, just the moment you have now. Make a commitment to live this moment in holiness and you will be on the road to becoming a saint!

Lord of true holiness, I do want to be holy. I want to be holy as You are holy. Help me to live each moment for You, with You and in You. I give this present moment to You, dear Lord. Jesus, I trust in You.

Second Week of Lent

Becoming White as Light

Second Sunday of Lent (Year A)

> Jesus took Peter, James, and John his brother, and led them up a high mountain by themselves. And he was transfigured before them; his face shone like the sun and his clothes became white as light. Matthew 17:1–2

What a fascinating line above: "white as light." How white is something that is "white as light?"

On this the second week of Lent, we are given the hopeful image of Jesus being transfigured before the eyes of Peter, James and John. They witness a small glimpse of His eternal glory and radiance as the Son of God and the Second Person of the Most Holy Trinity. They are stunned, in awe, amazed and filled with the greatest joy. Jesus' face shines like the sun and His clothing is so white, so pure, so radiant that they shine as the brightest and most pure light imaginable.

Why did this happen? Why did Jesus do this and why did He permit these three Apostles to see this glorious event? And to ponder further, why do we reflect upon this scene in the beginning of Lent?

Simply put, Lent is a time to examine our lives and to see our sins most clearly. It's a time we are given each year to pause from the confusion of life and to reexamine the road we are on. Looking at our sins can be hard. It can be depressing and can tempt us to depression, hopelessness and even despair. But the temptation to despair must be overcome. And it is not overcome by ignoring our sin, rather, it is overcome by turning our eyes to the power and glory of God.

The Transfiguration is an event given to these three Apostles to give them hope as they prepare to face the suffering and death of Jesus. They are given this glimpse of glory and hope as they prepare to see Jesus embrace their sins and endure the consequences.

If we face sin without hope, we are doomed. But if we face sin (our sin) with a remembrance of Who Jesus is and what He has done for us, then facing our sin will lead us not into despair but into victory and glory.

As the Apostles looked on and saw Jesus transfigured, they heard a voice from Heaven say, "This is my beloved Son, with whom I am well pleased; listen to him" (Mt. 17:5b). The Father spoke this of Jesus, but He also desires to speak it of each one of us. We need to see in the Transfiguration the end and goal of our lives. We need to know, with the deepest conviction, that the Father desires to transform us into the whitest light, lifting all sin, and bestowing upon us the great dignity of being a true son or daughter of Him.

Reflect, today, upon your sin. But do so as you also reflect upon the transfigured and glorious nature of our divine Lord. He came to bestow this gift of holiness on each one of us. This is our calling. This is our dignity. This is who we must become, and the only way to do so is to allow God to cleanse us of every sin in our lives and to draw us into His glorious life of grace.

My transfigured Lord, You shone in radiance before the eyes of Your Apostles so that they could testify to the beauty of the life to which we are all called. During this Lent, help me to face my sin with courage and confidence in You and in Your power to not only forgive but to also transform. My I die to sin more deeply than ever before so as to share more fully in the glory of Your divine life. Jesus, I trust in You.

Transfigured in Glory

Second Sunday of Lent (Year B)

> Jesus took Peter, James, and John and led them up a high mountain apart by themselves. And he was transfigured before them, and his clothes became dazzling white, such as no fuller on earth could bleach them. Mark 9:2–3

The many teachings of Jesus were hard for many to accept. His command to love your enemies, to take up your cross and follow Him, to lay down your life for another, and His call to perfection were demanding, to say the least. So as a help for all of us to embrace the challenges of the Gospel, Jesus chose Peter, James and John to receive a small vision of Who He truly is. He showed them a glimpse of His greatness and glory. And that image most certainly stayed with them and helped them every time they were tempted to get discouraged or despair over the holy demands our Lord placed upon them.

Recall that prior to the Transfiguration, Jesus taught His disciples that He would have to suffer and die and that they must also follow in His footsteps. So Jesus revealed to them a taste of His unimaginable glory. The glory and splendor of God is truly unimaginable. There is no way to comprehend His beauty, magnificence and splendor. Even in Heaven when we see Jesus face to face, we will eternally enter deeper and deeper into the incomprehensible mystery of God's glory.

Though we are not privileged to witness the image of His glory as these three Apostles were, their experience of this glory is given to us to ponder so that we will also receive the benefit of their experience. Since the glory and splendor of Christ is not just physical but also essentially a spiritual reality, He can give us a glimpse of His glory also. At times in life, Jesus will give us His consolation and instill within us a clear sense of Who He is. He will reveal to us through prayer a sense of Who He is, especially when we make the radical choice to follow Him without reserve. And though this may not be a daily experience, if you have ever received this gift by faith, then remind yourself of it when things get difficult in life.

Reflect, today, upon Jesus as He is now fully radiating His glory in Heaven. Recall that image whenever you find yourself tempted in life toward despair or doubt, or when you sense that Jesus simply wants too much of you. Remind yourself of Who Jesus truly is. Try to imagine what these Apostles saw and experienced. Allow their experience to become yours also, so that you will be able to daily make the choice to follow our Lord wherever He leads.

My transfigured Lord, You are truly glorious in a way that is beyond my comprehension. Your glory and splendor are beyond what my imagination can ever comprehend. Help me to always keep the eyes of my heart upon You and to allow the image of Your Transfiguration to strengthen me when I'm tempted to despair. I love You, my Lord, and place all my hope in You. Jesus, I trust in You.

Joy at the Transfiguration

Second Sunday of Lent (Year C)

> Peter said to Jesus, "Master, it is good that we are here; let us make three tents, one for you, one for Moses, and one for Elijah." Luke 9:33

Peter was excited, perhaps beyond any excitement he had experienced before. In fact, to say he was excited is most certainly an understatement. It may be more appropriate to say that he was overwhelmed! Why was this the case? Because he had just been given a very small glimpse of the glory and splendor of God!

This is the Transfiguration. Jesus took Peter, James and John and they went up a high mountain together. These three Apostles had no idea what was coming. Most likely while on the way they were complaining interiorly, wondering why they had to go up the mountain. But the mountain is a symbol of our upward journey to Heaven. It takes focus and drive, commitment and resolve to go there, and it's an elevated place, a place away from the ordinary occurrences of life.

So they were on this difficult climb up the mountain and suddenly they stopped in shock and awe. They saw before their eyes Jesus changed in a glorious way, His clothing being whiter than any white they had ever seen. And Moses and Elijah, the great Law-giver and the great Prophet, were there before them conversing with Jesus.

And what was going on in Peter's head? What was he experiencing? He was experiencing a small glimpse of the glory and splendor of God. Jesus, who up until this moment had kept His divinity veiled, lifted the veil ever so slightly. And with the lifting of that veil, His divinity shone through brighter than anything this world could ever contain. And Peter, James and John did not know what to think. But Peter cried out that he wanted to build three tents, one for Jesus, one for Moses and one for Elijah! For within that momentary experience, he experienced the desire to remain there forever.

So why did Jesus give these Apostles this very brief experience of His glory? Because they would need that taste of His goodness for the road ahead. They would need to forever remember what their final destiny was. They would need to hold this experience close as they endured the many crosses and sufferings ahead. And they would use this experience to remind themselves that whatever they had to endure on the journey up the mountain of life is worth it.

Because on the summit is a glory so great that no hardship they would have to endure would ever prove to be too big.

God wants to give that message to us through them. He wants us to ponder this experience they had and He wants us to try to enter into it so that we too can willingly press on during the journey.

Reflect, today, at the beginning of Lent, on the glory of God that makes the crosses we endure all worth it. Take advantage of this experience of Peter, James and John and try to make their experience your own. Be consoled by God's glory and never forget that this is the ultimate promise He gives to all who press on.

My transfigured Lord, may I be consoled by Your glory and splendor. May I believe in this glory and keep it ever in my mind as I press on through the hardships and challenges I face. You travel the road ahead of me and You will lead me on my journey if I only trust in You. Jesus, I do trust in You!

Judging the Actions, Not the Heart

Monday of the Second Week of Lent

> "Stop judging and you will not be judged. Stop condemning and you will not be condemned." Luke 6:37

Have you ever met someone for the first time and without even talking to this person suddenly came to the conclusion of what you think of them? Perhaps it was that they seemed a bit standoffish, or had a certain lack of expression, or seemed distracted. If we are honest with ourselves we'd have to admit that it's very easy to come to an immediate judgment of others. It's easy to immediately think that because they seem distant or standoffish, or lack that expression of warmth, or are distracted, that they must have a problem.

What's hard to do is to completely suspend our judgment of others. It's hard to immediately give them the benefit of the doubt and to presume only the best.

On the flip side, we may encounter people who are very good actors. They are smooth and courteous; they look us in the eye and smile, shake our hand and treat us in a very gracious way. You may walk away thinking, "Wow, that person really has it all together!"

The problem with both of these approaches is that it's really not our place to form a judgment for good or for ill in the first place. Perhaps the one who makes a good impression is simply a good "politician" and knows how to turn on the charm. But charm can be deceptive.

The key here, from Jesus' statement, is that we must strive to be non-judgmental in every way. It's simply not our place. God is the judge of the good and the bad. Sure we should look at good actions and be grateful when we see them and even offer affirmation for the goodness we see. And, sure, we should notice poor behavior, offer correction as needed, and do it with love. But judging the actions is much different than judging the person. We ought not judge the person, nor do we want to be judged or condemned by others. We do not want others to presume they know our hearts and motives.

Perhaps one important lesson we can take from this statement of Jesus is that the world needs more people who are non-judgmental and non-condemning. We need more people who know how to be true friends and love unconditionally. And God wants you to be one of those persons.

Reflect, today, upon how often you do judge others and reflect upon how good you are at offering the kind of friendship others around you need. In the end, if you offer this sort of friendship you will most likely be blessed with others who offer this sort of friendship right back! And with that you will both be blessed!

Lord, give me a non-judgmental heart. Help me to love each person I encounter with a holy love and acceptance. Help me to have the charity I need to correct their wrongdoing with kindness and firmness, but to also see beyond the surface and see the person You created. In turn, give me the true love and friendship of others so that I may trust and enjoy the love You wish me to have. Jesus, I trust in You.

The Exaltation of the Humble of Heart

Tuesday of the Second Week of Lent

> "Whoever exalts himself will be humbled; but whoever humbles himself will be exalted." Matthew 23:12

Humility seems like such a contradiction. We are easily tempted to think that the way to greatness involves letting everyone know all that we do well. There is a constant temptation for most people to put forward their best face and to hope others will see that and admire it. We want to be noticed and praised. And we often try to make that happen by the little things we do and say. And often we tend to exaggerate who we are.

On the flip side, if someone criticizes us and thinks ill of us it has the potential of being devastating. If we hear that someone said something negative about us we may go home and be depressed or angry about it the rest of the day, or even the rest of the week! Why? Because our pride is wounded and that wound can hurt. It can hurt unless we have discovered the incredible gift of humility.

Humility is a virtue that enables us to be real. It enables us to cut through any false persona we may have and simply be who we are. It enables us to be comfortable with our good qualities as well as our failures. Humility is nothing other than being honest and true about our lives and being comfortable with that person.

Jesus gives us a wonderful lesson in the Gospel passage above that is very hard to live but is absolutely key to living a happy life. He wants us to be exalted! He wants us to be noticed by others. He wants our light of goodness to shine for all to see and for that light to make a difference. But He wants it done in truth, not by presenting a false persona. He wants the real "me" to shine forth. And that is humility.

Humility is sincerity and genuineness. And when people see this quality in us they are impressed. Not so much in a worldly way but in an authentic human way. They will not look at us and be envious, rather, they will look at us and see the true qualities we have and enjoy them, admire them and want to imitate them. Humility enables the real you to shine through. And, believe it or not, the real you is someone who others want to meet and get to know.

Reflect, today, on how genuine you are. Make this time of Lent a time when the foolishness of pride is shattered. Let God strip away every false image of yourself so that the true you can shine forth. Humble yourself in this way and God will take you and exalt you in His way so that your heart can be seen and loved by those around you.

Lord of perfect humility, make me humble. Help me to be sincere and honest about who I am. And in that honesty, help me to let Your Heart, living in mine, shine through for others to see. Jesus, I trust in You.

The Life of Sacrifice

Wednesday of the Second Week of Lent

> Jesus said in reply, "You do not know what you are asking. Can you drink the chalice that I am going to drink?" They said to him, "We can." He replied, "My chalice you will indeed drink, but to sit at my right and at my left, this is not mine to give but is for those for whom it has been prepared by my Father." Matthew 20:22–23

It's easy to have good intentions, but is that enough? The Gospel passage above was spoken by Jesus to the brothers James and John after their loving mother came to Jesus and asked Him to promise her that her two sons would sit on His right and left when He took up His kingly throne. Perhaps it was a bit bold of her to ask that of Jesus, but it was clearly a mother's love that was behind her request.

However, it's important to note that she didn't actually realize what she was asking. And if she did realize what she was asking, she may not have asked Jesus for this "favor" at all. Jesus was going up to Jerusalem where He would take up His throne of the Cross and be crucified. And it was in this context that Jesus is asked if James and John could join Him on His *throne*. This is why Jesus asks these two Apostles, "Can you drink the chalice that I am going to drink?" To which they respond, "We can." And Jesus confirms this by telling them, "My chalice you will indeed drink."

They were invited by Jesus to follow in His footsteps and to courageously give their lives in a sacrificial way for the love of others. They were to abandon all fear and were to be ready and willing to say "Yes" to their own crosses as they sought to serve Christ and His mission.

Following Jesus is not something we ought to do half way. If we want to be a true follower of Christ then we, too, need to drink the chalice of His Precious Blood deep into our souls and to be nourished by that gift so that we are ready and willing to give of ourselves to the point of a total sacrifice. We need to be ready and willing to hold nothing back, even if that means the greatest of sacrifice.

True, very few people will be called to be *literal* martyrs, but we are ALL called to be martyrs in spirit. This means that we must be so completely given over to Christ and His will that we have died to ourselves.

Reflect, today, upon Jesus asking you this question, "Can you drink of the chalice that I am going to drink?" Can you willingly give everything, holding nothing back? Can your love of God and others be so complete and total that you are a martyr in the truest sense of the word? Resolve to say "Yes," drink the chalice of His Precious Blood and daily offer your life in total sacrifice. It's worth it and you can do it!

My sacrificial Lord, may my love for You and others be so complete that I hold nothing back. May I give my mind only to Your Truth and my will to Your Way. And may the gift of Your Precious Blood be my strength on this journey so that I may imitate Your perfect and sacrificial love. Jesus, I trust in You.

True Riches

Thursday of the Second Week of Lent

> When the poor man died, he was carried away by angels to the bosom of Abraham. The rich man also died and was buried, and from the netherworld, where he was in torment, he raised his eyes and saw Abraham far off and Lazarus at his side. Luke 16:22–23

If you had to choose, what would you prefer? To be rich and dine sumptuously every day, clothed in purple garments, having everything you could ever want in this world? Or to be a poor beggar, covered with sores, living in a doorway, feeling the pains of hunger? It's an easy question to answer on the surface. The rich and comfortable life is more attractive at first thought. But the question should not be considered only on the surface, we must look deeper and consider the full contrast of these two people and the effects that their inner lives have on their eternal souls.

As for the poor man, when he died "he was carried away by angels to the bosom of Abraham." As for the rich man, the Scripture states that he "died and was buried" and went to the "netherworld, where he was in torment." Now who would you prefer to be like?

Though it may be desirable to be rich in this life AND the next, that's not the point of Jesus' story. The point of His story is simple in that while on this Earth we must repent, turn from sin, listen to the words of Scripture, believe and keep our eyes on our true goal of the riches of Heaven.

As for whether you are rich or poor in this life, it really shouldn't matter. Though that's a hard conviction to arrive at, interiorly, it must be our goal. Heaven, and the riches that await, must be our focus. And we prepare for Heaven by hearing the Word of God and responding with the utmost generosity.

The rich man could have responded in this life by seeing the dignity and value of the poor man lying in his doorway, and reaching out in love and mercy. But he didn't. He was too focused on himself.

Reflect, today, upon the stark contrast between these two men, and especially the eternity that awaited each of them. If you see any of the sinful tendencies of this rich man in your own life, then repent of these sins and repent today.

See the dignity and value in each person you encounter. And if you tend to be more focused upon your own self, consumed with selfish pleasure and excess, seek to embrace true poverty of spirit, striving to be attached only to God and the abundant blessings that come with a full embrace of all that He has revealed to us.

Lord of true riches, please free me from my selfishness. Help me, instead, to remain focused upon the dignity of all people and to pour myself out in their service. May I discover in the poor, the broken and the humble, an image of You. And as I discover Your presence in their lives, may I love You, in them, seeking to be an instrument of Your mercy. Jesus, I trust in You.

Rejection Transformed

Friday of the Second Week of Lent

> The stone that the builders rejected has become the cornerstone. Matthew 21:42

Of all the rejections that have been experienced throughout the ages, there is one that stands out above the rest. It's the rejection of the Son of God. Jesus had nothing other than pure and perfect love in His Heart. He wanted the absolute best for everyone He encountered. And He was willing to offer the gift of His life to whoever would accept it. Though many have accepted it, many have also rejected it.

It's important to understand that the rejection Jesus experienced left deep pain and suffering. Certainly the actual Crucifixion was extraordinarily painful. But the wound He experienced in His Heart from the rejection of so many was His greatest pain and caused the greatest of suffering.

Suffering in this sense was an act of love, not an act of weakness. Jesus didn't suffer interiorly because of pride or a poor self image. Rather, His Heart hurt because He loved so deeply. And when that love was rejected, it filled Him with the holy sorrow spoken of in the Beatitudes ("Blessed are they who mourn..." Matthew 5:4). This sort of sorrow was not a form of despair; rather, it was a deep experience of the loss of the love of another. It was holy, and a result of His burning love for all.

When we experience rejection it is hard to sort out the pain we feel. It's *very* hard to let the hurt and anger we feel turn into a "holy sorrow" which has the effect of motivating us toward a deeper love of those whom we mourn over. This is difficult to do but is what our Lord did. The result of Jesus doing this was the salvation of the world. Imagine if Jesus would have simply given up. What if, at the time of His arrest, Jesus would have called on the myriads of angels to come to His rescue. What if He would have done this thinking, "These people are not worth it!" The result would have been that we would have never received the eternal gift of salvation by His death and Resurrection. Suffering would not have been transformed into love.

Reflect, today, upon the deep truth that rejection is potentially one of the greatest gifts we have to fight against evil. It's "potentially" one of the greatest gifts because it all depends on how we ultimately respond. Jesus responded with perfect love when he cried out, "Father, forgive them, they know not what they do." This act of perfect love in the midst of His ultimate rejection enabled Him to become the "Cornerstone" of the Church and, therefore, the Cornerstone of new life! We are called to imitate this love and to share in His ability to not only forgive, but to also offer the holy love of mercy. When we do, we also will become a cornerstone of love and grace for those who need it the most.

Lord of mercy, help me to be that cornerstone. Help me to not only forgive every time I'm hurt, but let me also offer love and mercy in return. You are the divine and perfect example of this love. May I share in this same love, crying out with You, "Father, forgive them, they know not what they do." Jesus, I trust in You.

A Father's Unwavering Love
Saturday of the Second Week of Lent

> "Quickly, bring the finest robe and put it on him; put a ring on his finger and sandals on his feet. Take the fattened calf and slaughter it. Then let us celebrate with a feast, because this son of mine was dead, and has come to life again; he was lost, and has been found." Then the celebration began. Luke 15:22–24

In this familiar story of the Prodigal Son, we see courage in the son by choosing to return to his father. And this is significant even though the son returned primarily out of desperate need. Yes, he humbly admits his wrongs and asks his father to forgive and to treat him like one of his hired hands. But he did return! The question to answer is "Why?"

It's fair to say that the son returned to the father, first and foremost, because he *knew in his heart* the goodness of his father. The father was a good father. He had shown his love and care for his son throughout his life. And even though the son rejected the father, it doesn't change the fact that the son always knew he was loved by him. Perhaps he didn't even realize how much he actually realized this. But it was this certain realization in his heart that gave him the courage to return to his father with hope in the father's abiding love.

This reveals that authentic love always works. It is always effective. Even if someone rejects the holy love we offer, it always has an impact upon them. True unconditional love is hard to ignore and it's hard to push away. The son realized this lesson and so must we.

Spend time prayerfully pondering the father's heart. We should ponder the hurt he must have felt but also look at the constant hope he must have had as he anticipated his son's return. We should ponder the overflowing joy in his heart as he saw his son returning from a distance. He ran to him, ordered he be well taken care of, and had a party. These things are all signs of a love that cannot be contained.

This is the love the Father in Heaven has for each of us. He is not an angry or harsh God. He is a God who longs to take us back and reconcile with us. He wishes to rejoice the moment we turn to Him in our need. Even if we are uncertain, He is certain about His love, He is always waiting for us, and deep down we all know that.

Reflect, today upon the importance of reconciling with the Father in Heaven. Lent is an ideal time for the Sacrament of Reconciliation. That Sacrament is this story. It's the story of us going to the Father with our sin and Him lavishing us with His mercy. It may be frightening and intimidating to go to Confession, but if we enter into that Sacrament with honesty and sincerity, we are in for a wonderful surprise. God will run to us, lift our burdens and put them behind us. Don't let this Lent go by without participating in this wonderful gift of the Sacrament of Reconciliation.

Compassionate Father, I do sin. I have turned away from You and acted on my own. Now is the time to return to You with an open and honest heart. Give me the courage I need to embrace that love in the Sacrament of Reconciliation. Thank You for Your unwavering and perfect love. Father in Heaven, Holy Spirit, and Jesus my Lord, I trust in You.

Third Week of Lent

Quenching Your Thirst with Living Water

Third Sunday of Lent (Year A)

(Note: This Gospel is also optional for Years B & C with Scrutinies)

> "Come see a man who told me everything I have done. Could he possibly be the Christ?" John 4:29

This is the story of a woman who encountered Jesus at the well. She comes to the well in the middle of the noonday heat so as to avoid the other women of her town for fear of encountering their judgment upon her, for she was a sinful woman. At the well she encounters Jesus. Jesus speaks with her for a while and she is deeply touched by this casual but transforming conversation.

The first thing to note is that the very fact of Jesus speaking to her touched her. She was a Samaritan woman and Jesus was a Jewish man. Jewish men did not speak to Samaritan women. But there was something more that Jesus said that deeply affected her. As the woman herself tells us, He "told me everything I have done."

She wasn't only impressed that Jesus knew all about her past as if He were a mind reader or magician. There is more to this encounter than the simple fact that Jesus told her all about her past sins. What truly seemed to touch her was that within the context of Jesus knowing all about her, all the sins of her past life and her broken relationships, He still treated her with the greatest respect and dignity. This was a new experience for her!

We can be certain that she would have daily experienced a sort of community shame. The way she lived in the past and the way she was living at the present was not an acceptable lifestyle. And she felt the shame of it which, as mentioned above, was the reason she came to the well in the middle of the day. She was avoiding others.

But here was Jesus. He knew all about her but wanted to give her Living Water nonetheless. He wanted to satiate the thirst that she was feeling in her soul. As He spoke to her, and as she experienced His gentleness and acceptance, that thirst began to be quenched. It began to be quenched because what she really needed, what we all need, is this perfect love and acceptance that Jesus offers. He offered it to her, and He offers it to us.

Interestingly, the woman went away and "left her water jar" by the well. She never actually got the water she came for. Or did she? Symbolically, this act of leaving the water jar at the well is a sign that her thirst was quenched by this encounter with Jesus. She was no longer thirsty, at least spiritually speaking. Jesus, the Living Water, satiated.

Reflect, today, upon the undeniable thirst that is within you. Once you are aware of it, make the conscious choice to let Jesus satiate it with Living Water. If you do this, you too will leave the many "jars" behind that never satisfy for very long.

Jesus, You are the Living Water that my soul needs. May I meet You in the heat of my day, in the trials of life, and in my shame and guilt. May I encounter Your love, gentleness and acceptance in these moments, and may that Love become the source of my new life in You. Jesus, I trust in You.

The Holy Wrath of God

Third Sunday of Lent (Year B)

> He made a whip out of cords and drove them all out of the temple area, with the sheep and oxen, and spilled the coins of the money-changers and overturned their tables, and to those who sold doves he said, "Take these out of here, and stop making my Father's house a marketplace." John 2:15–16

Jesus made quite a scene. He directly engaged those who were turning the Temple into a marketplace. Those selling animals for sacrifice were doing so as a way of trying to make a profit off of the sacred practices of the Jewish faith. They were not there to serve the will of God; rather, they were there to serve themselves. And this brought forth the holy wrath of our Lord.

It's important to point out that Jesus' wrath was not the result of Him losing His temper. It was not the result of His out of control emotions pouring forth in extreme anger. No, Jesus was fully in control of Himself and exercised His wrath as a result of a powerful passion of love. In this case, His perfect love was manifested through the passion of anger.

Anger is normally understood as a sin and it is sinful when it's the result of one losing control. But it's important to note that the passion of anger, in and of itself, is not sinful. A passion is a powerful drive which manifests itself in various ways. The key question to ask is, "What is driving that passion?"

In Jesus' case, it was hatred for sin and love for the sinner that drove Him to this holy wrath. By turning over the tables and driving people out of the Temple with a whip, Jesus made it clear that He loved His Father, whose house they were in, and He loved the people enough to passionately rebuke the sin that they were committing. The ultimate goal of His action was their conversion.

Jesus hates the sin in your life with the same perfect passion. At times we need a holy rebuke to set us on the correct path. Do not be afraid to let the Lord offer this form of rebuke to you this Lent.

Reflect, today, upon those parts of your life that Jesus wants to cleanse. Allow Him to speak directly and firmly to you so that you will be driven to repentance. The Lord loves you with a perfect love and desires that all sin in your life be cleansed.

My passionate Lord, I know that I am a sinner who is in need of Your mercy and, at times, in need of Your holy wrath. Help me to humbly receive Your rebukes of love and to allow You to drive all sin from my life. Have mercy on me, dear Lord. Please have mercy. Jesus, I trust in You.

Exhausting the "Soil" of Mercy

Third Sunday of Lent (Year C)

> "Sir, leave it for this year also, and I shall cultivate the ground around it and fertilize it; it may bear fruit in the future. If not you can cut it down." Luke 13:8–9

Every gardener knows that good fruit is, in part, dependent upon the presence of good soil. But other factors are also important in the production of good fruit. The plant must be free of disease, receive water and sun, be planted in a warm environment, be properly pruned, and have enough space to grow. When all factors are present, good fruit is guaranteed.

So it is with our lives. The soil in which we are to be planted is the mercy of God. And this soil is the richest soil attainable for the production of the virtues in our lives. God also produces the sun, the rain, and the warmth that is needed for our growth. But, analogously speaking, we must allow ourselves to be pruned. We must also allow the soil to be fertilized and cultivated in a variety of ways. Though Jesus is the Gardener of our lives, it's also fair to say that we are the gardeners in the sense that we must cooperate with our Lord, relying upon the supernatural resources of the Creator to ensure the healthy growth of our spiritual lives so that the good fruit of virtue may be born in our lives.

This passage above is the conclusion to the Parable of the Fig Tree. Just prior to this passage, the owner of the vineyard, God the Father, ordered that the barren fig tree be cut down so that it will no longer exhaust the soil. But our merciful Lord, sent on mission from the Father to till the soil of our lives, seeks to offer one more chance and the Father obliges out of love. This life is that "year" by which our Lord works fervently to cultivate the soil around us. We must cooperate through daily prayer, fidelity to His commands, acts of loving sacrifice and surrender to His providence. In the end, if we allow our Lord to do all He desires, our lives will bear good fruit.

But on the flip side, make no mistake about the fact that, if our lives do not bear good fruit, we will be "cut down." Bearing good fruit is not an option, it's a must. It's a clear indication of our spiritual health and it will become the measure of our eternal reward or eternal death. Do not be intimidated by such sharp language coming from our Lord. He spoke it in love so that we will know the serious duty we have to bear good fruit in our lives.

Reflect, today, upon the outward signs of your inward spiritual health. Do you see the virtues sprouting forth from your life? Are you aware of the work God desires to do in your soul so as to cultivate it and fertilize it with grace and mercy? Say "Yes" to Him this day and allow that grace to produce an abundance of good fruit.

My virtuous Lord, I invite You into my soul to cultivate it and fertilize it with Your grace. Please prune my sins and help me to sink my roots deeply into the nourishment of Your mercy. I am sorry for the ways that I have failed to bear fruit in my life. I now entrust myself to You so that Your care will remedy all my ills and weaknesses. Jesus, I trust in You.

Athirst My Soul!

Monday of the Third Week of Lent

> Athirst is my soul for the living God. When shall I go and behold the face of God? (See Psalm 42:3)

What a beautiful statement to be able to make. The word "athirst" is a word not used that often but worth reflecting on all by itself. It reveals a longing and a desire to be quenched not only by God, but by the "Living God!" And to "behold the face of God."

How often do you long for such a thing? How often do you let the desire for God burn within your soul? This is a wonderful desire and longing to have. In fact, the desire itself is enough to begin bringing great satisfaction and fulfillment in life.

There is a story of an elderly monk who lived his life as a hermit being a priest and chaplain for a group of monastic sisters. This monk lived a very quiet life of solitude, prayer, study and work most of his life. One day, toward the end of his life, he was asked how he enjoyed his life all these years. Immediately and without hesitation his face became radiant and overwhelmed with a deep joy. And he said with the deepest of conviction, "What a glorious life I have! Every day I'm preparing to die."

Third Week of Lent

This monk had one focus in life. It was a focus on the face of God. Nothing else really mattered. What he longed for and anticipated each and every day was that moment when he would enter into that glorious Beatific Vision and see God face to face. And it was the thought of this that enabled him to press on, day after day, year after year, offering Mass and worshiping God in preparation for that glorious meeting.

What do you thirst for? How would you complete that statement? "Athirst is my soul for…?" For what? Too often we thirst for those things that are so artificial and temporary. We try so hard to be happy and yet we so often fall short. But if we can let our hearts be inflamed with longing for that which is essential, that which we were made for, then everything else in life will fall into place. If God is placed at the center of all our longings, all our hopes and all our desires, we will actually begin to "behold the face of God" here and now. Even the slightest glimpse of God's glory will satiate us so much that it will transform our whole outlook on life and give us a clear and certain direction in all we do. Every relationship will be affected, every decision we make will be orchestrated by the Holy Spirit, and the purpose and meaning of life we are searching for will be discovered. Every time we think about our lives we will become radiant as we ponder the journey we are on and long to put it into full motion anticipating the eternal reward awaiting us in the end.

Reflect, today, upon your "thirst." Don't waste your life on empty promises. Don't get caught up in earthly attachments. Seek God. Seek His face. Seek His will and His glory and you will never want to turn back from the direction this longing takes you.

Jesus, my Living God, may I one day behold Your full splendor and glory. May I see Your face and make that goal the center of my life.

May everything I am be caught up in this burning desire, and may I bask in the joy of this journey. Jesus, I trust in You.

Forgiving and Being Forgiven
Tuesday of the Third Week of Lent

> The servant fell down, did him homage, and said, "Be patient with me, and I will pay you back in full." Moved with compassion the master of that servant let him go and forgave him the loan. Matthew 18:26–27

This is a story about giving and receiving forgiveness. Interestingly, it's often easier to forgive than it is to ask forgiveness. Sincerely asking for forgiveness requires that you honestly acknowledge your sin, which is hard to do. It's hard to take responsibility for what we have done wrong.

In this parable, the man asking patience with his debt appears to be sincere. He "fell down" before his master asking for mercy and patience. And the master responded with mercy by forgiving him the entire debt which was more than the servant had even requested.

But was the servant truly sincere or was he just a good actor? It seems that he was a good actor because as soon as he was forgiven this huge debt, he ran into someone else who actually owed him money and instead of showing the same forgiveness he was shown, "He seized him and started to choke him, demanding, 'Pay back what you owe.'"

Forgiveness, if it is real, must affect everything about us. It is something that we must ask for, give, receive, and give again. Here are a few points for you to consider:

> Can you honestly see your sin, experience sorrow for that sin, and say, "I'm sorry" to another?

When you are forgiven, what does that do to you? Does it have the effect of making you more merciful toward others?

Can you in turn offer the same level of forgiveness and mercy that you hope to receive from God and others?

If you cannot answer "Yes" to all of these questions then this story was written for you. It was written for you to help you grow more in the gifts of mercy and forgiveness. These are hard questions to face but they are essential questions to face if we want to be freed of the burdens of anger and resentment. Anger and resentment weigh heavily on us and God wants us freed of them.

Reflect, today, upon these questions above and prayerfully examine your actions. If you find any resistance to these questions, then focus on what strikes you, take it to prayer, and let God's grace enter in to bring about a deeper conversion in that area of your life.

Merciful Lord, I do acknowledge my sin. But I acknowledge it in the light of Your abundant grace and mercy. As I receive that mercy in my life, please make me just as merciful toward others. Help me to offer forgiveness freely and fully, holding nothing back. Jesus, I trust in You.

The Timing of God

Wednesday of the Third Week of Lent

Jesus said to his disciples: "Do not think that I have come to abolish the law or the prophets. I have come not to abolish but to fulfill." Matthew 5:17

Sometimes God seems to move slowly...very slowly. Perhaps we've all found it hard to be patient with the timing of God in our lives. It's easy to think that we know best and if we only pray harder, then we will push God's hand and

He will finally act, doing what we pray for. But this is not the way God works.

The Scripture above should give us some insight into God's ways. They are slow, steady, and perfect. Jesus refers to the "law and the prophets" stating that He came not to abolish them but to fulfill them. This is true. But it's worth looking carefully how this came about.

It came about over many thousands of years. It took time for the perfect plan of God to unfold. But it did unfold in His time and in His way. Perhaps all those in the Old Testament were anxious for the Messiah to come and to fulfill all things. But prophet after prophet came and went and continued to point to the future coming of the Messiah. Even the Old Testament law was a way of preparing God's people for the coming of the Messiah. But again, it was a slow process of forming the law, implementing it for the people of Israel, enabling them to understand it, and then beginning to live it.

Even when the Messiah finally did come, there were many who, in their excitement and zeal, wanted Him to fulfill all things right then and there. They wanted their earthly kingdom to be established and they wanted their newfound Messiah to take up His Kingdom!

But God's plan was so very different than human wisdom. His ways were far above our ways. And His ways continue to be far above our ways! Jesus fulfilled every part of the Old Testament law and prophets, just not in the way many were expecting.

What does this teach us? It teaches us lots of patience. And it teaches us surrender, trust and hope. If we want to pray hard and pray well, we need to pray correctly. And the correct way to pray is to continually pray that Thy **will be done!** Again, this is hard at first, but it becomes easy when we understand and believe that God always has the perfect plan for our lives and for every struggle and situation in which we find ourselves.

Reflect, today, upon your patience and your trust in the ways of the Lord. He has a perfect plan for your life, and that plan is most likely different than your plan. Surrender to Him and let His holy will guide you in all things.

My perfect Lord, I entrust my life to You. I trust that You have the perfect plan for me and for all Your beloved children. Give me patience to wait upon You and to let You bring Your divine will to fulfillment in my life. Jesus, I trust in You!

Speaking the Word of God, Freely
Thursday of the Third Week of Lent

> Jesus was driving out a demon that was mute, and when the demon had gone out, the mute man spoke and the crowds were amazed. Luke 11:14

What hinders you from speaking the Word of God openly, honestly and clearly? There are so many people who are in dire need of the Gospel. There are so many people who are confused in life and find themselves walking down the wrong road, a road leading to greater confusion and destruction. And we remain silent as they travel this road. Why?

The Gospel above speaks of a man who was mute as a result of a demon. When this demon was driven out by Jesus, the mute man spoke and many were amazed. Most likely this man was fully possessed by this demon and the oppression he experienced disabled his ability to even speak. Upon his release from this demonic influence, he spoke freely.

Though we may not experience demonic influence to the same degree, we are often hindered and oppressed by similar mute spirits. The evil one often tries to influence us in such a way that we are fearful of proclaiming the Gospel freely, sincerely and immediately to those who are in most need of the message God wants communicated to them. "Mute spirits" can often hinder us, confuse us or fill us with a certain fear when the opportunity arises to share our faith with another. Though it may be rare to fall completely into their power, we are often left influenced and hindered by them nonetheless.

Reflect, today, upon the reality of these vile spirits and their attempts to silence us, keeping us from speaking the message of truth that so many people need to hear. We ought not fear their influence. Jesus has complete power over all such spirits and will not hesitate to silence their influence over us if we let Him. He wants to free us to speak His message of love without reserve so that others will come to know Him and His perfect love. Let Him use you as one such instrument of truth and love.

Eternal Word of God, at times I am given over to fear when You call me to speak Your words of love to those in need. I feel as though I am muted in my speech, confused about what to say. Please free me, dear Lord, to be a holy instrument of Your Word and to confidently proclaim Your truth to those who are in much need. Jesus, I trust in You.

Don't Wait to Accomplish the Greatest Act!

Friday of the Third Week of Lent

> One of the scribes came to Jesus and asked him, "Which is the first of all the commandments?" Jesus replied, "The first is this: Hear, O Israel! The Lord our God is Lord alone! You shall love the Lord your God with all your heart, with all your soul, with all your mind, and with all your strength." Mark 12:28–30

It shouldn't come as a surprise to you that the greatest act you can do in life is to love God with your whole being. That is, to love Him with your whole heart, soul, mind and strength. Loving God above all things, with all the power of your human abilities, is the constant goal you must strive for in life. But what does that exactly mean?

First, this commandment of love identifies various aspects of who we are so as to emphasize that each aspect of our being must be given over to a total love of God. Philosophically speaking, we can identify these various aspects of our whole being as follows: intellect, will, passions, feelings, emotions and desires. How do we love God with all of these?

We start with our minds. The first step in loving God is coming to know Him. This means we must seek to understand, comprehend and believe in God and all that has been revealed to us about Him. It means we have sought to penetrate the very mystery of God's life, especially through Scripture and through the countless revelations given through the history of the Church.

Second, when we come to a deeper understanding of God and all that He has revealed, we make a free choice to believe in Him and follow His ways. This free choice must follow our knowledge of Him and becomes an act of faith in Him.

Third, when we have begun to penetrate the mystery of the life of God and chosen to believe in Him and all that He has revealed, we will see our lives change. One specific aspect of our lives that will change is that we will desire God and His will in our lives, we will want to seek Him more, we will find joy in following Him and we will discover that all the powers of our human soul will slowly become consumed with a love of Him and His ways.

Reflect, today, especially upon the first aspect of loving God. Reflect upon how diligently you seek to know and understand Him and all that He has revealed. This knowledge must become the foundation for your love with your whole being. Start with that and allow all else to follow. One way to do this is to begin a study of our entire Catholic faith (see: www.mycatholic.life).

My revealing Lord, I realize that in order to love You above all else I must come to know You. Help me to be diligent in my commitment to know You and to seek to discover all the glorious truths of Your life. I thank You for all that You have revealed to me and I dedicate myself, this day, to a more thorough discovery of Your life and revelation. Jesus, I trust in You.

Letting Go of Pride
Saturday of the Third Week of Lent

"Two people went up to the temple area to pray; one was a Pharisee and the other was a tax collector. The Pharisee took up his position and spoke this prayer to himself, 'O God, I thank you that I am not like the rest of humanity—greedy, dishonest, adulterous—or even like this tax collector.'" Luke 18:10–11

Pride and self-righteousness are quite ugly. This Gospel contrasts the Pharisee and his self-righteousness with the humility of the tax collector. The Pharisee looks righteous on the outside and is even proud enough to speak about how good he is in his prayer to God when he says that he is grateful he is not like the rest of humanity. That poor Pharisee. Little does he know that he is quite blind to the truth.

The tax collector, however, is truthful, humble and sincere. He cried out, "Oh God, be merciful to me a sinner." Jesus makes it clear that the tax collector, with this humble prayer, went home justified but the Pharisee did not.

When we witness the sincerity and humility of another it touches us. It's an inspiring sight to see. It's hard to criticize anyone who expresses their sinfulness and asks for forgiveness. Humility of this sort can win over even the most hardened of hearts.

So what about you? Is this parable addressed to you? Do you carry the heavy burden of self-righteousness? All of us do at least to some extent. It's hard to sincerely arrive at the level of humility that this tax collector had. And it's so very easy to fall into the trap of justifying our own sin and, as a result, becoming defensive and self-absorbed. But this is all pride. Pride disappears when we do two things well.

First, we have to understand God's mercy. Understanding the mercy of God frees us to take our eyes off ourselves and set aside self-righteousness and self-justification. It frees us from being defensive and enables us to see ourselves in the light of the truth. Why? Because when we recognize God's mercy for what it is, we also realize that even our sins cannot keep us from God. In fact, the greater the sinner, the more that sinner is deserving of God's mercy! So understanding God's mercy actually enables us to acknowledge our sin.

Acknowledging our sin is the second important step we must take if we want our pride to disappear. We have to know that it's OK to admit our sin. No, we do not have to stand on the street corner and tell everyone about the details of our sin. But we have to acknowledge it to ourselves and to God, especially in the confessional. And, at times, it will be necessary to acknowledge our sins to others so that we can ask for their forgiveness and mercy. This depth of humility is attractive and easily wins the hearts of others. It inspires and produces the good fruits of peace and joy in our hearts.

So do not be afraid to follow the example of this tax collector. Try to take his prayer today and say it over and over. Let it become your prayer and you will see the good fruits of this prayer in your life!

Oh God, be merciful to me a sinner. Oh God, be merciful to me a sinner. Oh God, be merciful to me a sinner. Jesus, I trust in You.

Fourth Week of Lent

Grace from the Ordinary

Fourth Sunday of Lent (Year A)

(Note: This Gospel is also optional for Years B & C with Scrutinies)

> As Jesus passed by he saw a man blind from birth…
>
> …he spat on the ground and made clay with the saliva, and smeared the clay on his eyes, and said to him, "Go wash in the Pool of Siloam" —which means Sent—. So he went and washed, and came back able to see. John 9:1, 6–7

Who was this man? Interestingly, he does not have a name. He is only referred to as the "man blind from birth." This is significant in the Gospel of John because the lack of a name is also seen, for example, in the story of "the woman at the well." The fact that there is no name indicates that we should see ourselves in this story.

"Blindness" is our inability to see the hand of God at work all around us. We struggle to see the daily miracles of God's grace alive in our lives and alive in the lives of others. So the first thing we should do with this Scripture is strive to see our lack of sight. We should strive to realize that we so often do not see God at work. This realization will inspire us to desire a spiritual healing. It will invite us to want to see God at work.

The good news is obviously that Jesus cured this man, as He willingly cures us. To restore sight is easy for Jesus. So the first prayer we should pray as a result of this story is simply, "Lord, I want to see!" The humble realization of our blindness will invite God's grace to work. And if we do not humbly acknowledge our blindness, we will not be in a position to seek healing.

How He heals this man is also significant. He uses His own spit to make mud and smear it on this man's eyes, which is not immediately that appealing. But it does reveal something quite significant to us. Namely, it reveals the fact that Jesus can use something exceptionally ordinary as a source of His divine grace!

If we look at this in a symbolic way we can come to some profound conclusions. Too often we look for God's action in the extraordinary. But He so often is present to us in that which is ordinary. Perhaps we will be tempted to think that God only works His grace through heroic acts of love or sacrifice. Perhaps we are tempted to think that God is not able to use our daily ordinary activities to perform His miracles. But this is not true. It is precisely those ordinary actions of life where God is present. He is present while washing the dishes, doing chores, driving a child to school, playing a game with a family member, carrying on a casual conversation or offering a helping hand. In fact, the more ordinary the activity, the more we should strive to see God at work. And when we do "see" Him at work in the ordinary activities of life, we will be healed of our spiritual blindness.

Reflect, today, upon this act of Jesus and allow our Lord to smear His spit and dirt on your eyes. Allow Him to give you the gift of spiritual sight. And as you begin to see His presence in your life, you will be amazed at the beauty you behold.

My miraculous Lord, I want to see. Help me to be healed of my blindness. Help me to see You at work in every ordinary activity of my life. Help me to see Your divine grace in the smallest events of my day. And as I see You alive and active, fill my heart with gratitude for this vision. Jesus, I trust in You.

A Summary of the Whole Gospel

Fourth Sunday of Lent (Year B)

> "For God so loved the world that he gave his only Son, so that everyone who believes in him might not perish but might have eternal life." John 3:16

This Scripture passage from John's Gospel is a familiar one. Oftentimes, at large public events such as sports games, we can find someone holding up a sign that says, "John: 3:16." The reason for this is that this passage offers a simple but clear summary of the entire Gospel.

There are four basic truths that we can take from this Scripture. Let's look at each of them in a brief way.

First, it's made clear that the Father in Heaven loves us. We know this but we will never fully comprehend the depth of this truth. God the Father loves us with a profound and perfect love. It's a love that is deeper than anything else we could ever experience in life. His love is perfect.

Second, the Father's love was made manifest by the gift of His Son Jesus. It is a profound act of love for the Father to give us His Son. The Son meant everything to the Father, and the gift of the Son to us means that the Father gives us everything. He gives His very life to us in the Person of Jesus.

Third, the only appropriate response we can make to such a gift is faith. We must believe in the transforming power of accepting the Son into our lives. We must see this gift as a gift that gives us all we need. We must accept the Son into our lives by believing in His mission and giving our lives to Him in return.

Fourth, the result of receiving Him and giving our lives in return is that we are saved. We will not perish in our sin; rather, we will be given eternal life. There is no other way to salvation than through the Son. We must know, believe, accept and embrace this truth.

Reflect, today, upon this summary of the entire Gospel. Read it over and over and memorize it. Savor every word and know that in embracing this short passage of Scripture you are embracing the entire truth of God.

Father in Heaven, I thank You for the perfect gift of Christ Jesus Your Son. By giving Jesus to us, You give us Your very Heart and Soul. May I be open to You more fully and to the perfect gift of Jesus in my life. I believe in You, my God. Please increase my faith and love. Jesus, I trust in You.

Coming to Your Senses
Fourth Sunday of Lent (Year C)

> Coming to his senses he thought, "How many of my father's hired workers have more than enough food to eat, but here am I, dying from hunger. I shall get up and go to my father and I shall say to him, 'Father, I have sinned against heaven and against you. I no longer deserve to be called your son; treat me as you would treat one of your hired workers.'" Luke 15:17–19

Why do we cling to our sins? This passage comes from the story of the Prodigal Son. We should know that story well. The son decided to leave his father and take his future inheritance, spending it on a life of sin. When the money he had ran out, he was in desperate need. So what did he do? He came to his senses!

This line alone is worth our meditation. First, it reveals what happens to a person who falls into a life of sin. In this case, the son eventually reaped the fruit of his sin. He found that his sin left him destitute and alone. He didn't know where

Fourth Week of Lent

to turn. And though our sins may not be to the extent of this son, we will all experience the empty effects of the sins we commit, just as this son did.

The profound insight we can gain from this son is that he did come around. Specifically, by "coming to his senses" he recognized two important things. First, he realized that he is worth more than a life of destitution. No one should have to live an impoverished and empty life. Therefore, by seeing his own dignity he came to realize that he was made for more.

Secondly, he knew he could turn to his father. What a blessing it was for him to know this. The reason he knew he could turn to his father was that his father clearly loved him with unconditional love. The mercy in the heart of the father was so strong that the son was aware of it and this awareness gave him confidence to turn to him.

Reflect, today, upon this twofold action. The son sees his misery and also sees his father as the person to whom he can confidently turn. We must strive to do the same in our own lives. The Father in Heaven will never reject us. No matter what we have done or how far we have turned away, the Father's love is perfect, relentless, unconditional and always inviting. He is ready and willing to dismiss every wrong we have done if we only turn to Him in confidence. Come to your senses in regard to your sins! Let go of them, repent and trust in the mercy of God.

Lord of perfect love, my sins do leave me dry and empty inside. I see the misery and pain that result from the sinful choices I have made. Help me, dear Lord, to come to my senses and to turn from every sin I commit. Help me to see that Your mercy is far greater than anything I have done. I thank You for Your perfect love and turn to You in my need. Jesus, I trust in You.

An Interesting Miracle

Monday of the Fourth Week of Lent

> Jesus said to him, "Unless you people see signs and wonders, you will not believe." The royal official said to him, "Sir, come down before my child dies." Jesus said to him, "You may go; your son will live." John 4:48–50

Indeed the child does live and the royal official is overjoyed when he returns home to find that his child was healed. This healing took place at the same time that Jesus said he would be healed.

One interesting thing to note about this passage is the contrast of Jesus' words. At first, it almost sounds as if Jesus is angry when He says, "Unless you people see signs and wonders, you will not believe." But then He immediately heals the boy telling the man, "Your son will live." Why this apparent contrast in Jesus' words and action?

We should note that Jesus' initial words are not so much a criticism; rather, they are simply words of truth. He is aware of the fact that many people lack faith, or are at least weak in faith. He is also aware of the fact that "signs and wonders" are beneficial for people at times so as to help them come to believe. Though this need to see "signs and wonders" is far from ideal, Jesus works with it. He uses this desire for a miracle as a way of offering faith.

What's important to understand is that the ultimate goal of Jesus was not the physical healing, even though this was an act of great love; rather, His ultimate goal was to increase the faith of this father by offering him the gift of his son's healing. This is important to understand because everything we experience in life from our Lord will have as its goal a deepening of our faith. Sometimes that takes on the form of "signs and wonders" while at other times it may be His sustaining presence in the midst of a trial without any visible sign or wonder. The goal we must strive for is *faith* by allowing whatever our Lord does in our lives to become the source of our faith's increase.

Reflect, today, upon your own level of faith and trust. And work to discern the actions of God in your life so that those actions produce greater faith. Cling to Him, believe He loves you, know that He holds the answer you need and seek Him in all things. He will never let you down.

My loving Lord, please increase my faith. Help me to see You acting in my life and to discover Your perfect love in all things. As I see You at work in my life, help me to know, with greater certainty, Your perfect love. Jesus, I trust in You.

Paralyzed by Sin

Tuesday of the Fourth Week of Lent

> Jesus said to him, "Rise, take up your mat, and walk." Immediately the man became well, took up his mat, and walked. John 5:8–9

Let's look at one of the clear symbolic meanings of this passage above. The man Jesus healed was paralyzed, being unable to walk and take care of himself. Others neglected him as he sat there by the pool, hoping for kindness and attention. Jesus sees him and gives him His full attention. After a short dialogue, Jesus cures him and tells him to rise and walk.

One clear symbolic message is that his physical paralysis is an image of the result of sin in our lives. When we sin we "paralyze" ourselves. Sin has grave consequences on our lives and the clearest consequence is that we are left unable to rise and then walk in the ways of God. Grave sin, especially, renders us powerless to love and live in true freedom. It leaves us trapped and unable to care for our own spiritual lives or for others in any way. It's important to see the consequences of sin. Even minor sins hinder our abilities, strip us of energy, and leave us spiritually crippled to one extent or another.

Hopefully you know this and it is not a new revelation to you. But what must be new to you is the honest admission of your current guilt. You must see yourself in this story. Jesus did not heal this man only for the good of this one man. He healed him, in part, to tell you that He sees you in your broken state as you experience the consequences of your sin. He sees you in need, looks at you and calls you to rise and walk. Do not underestimate the importance of allowing Him to perform a healing in your life. Do not neglect to identify even the smallest sin which imposes its consequences upon you. Look at your sin, allow Jesus to see it, and listen to Him speak words of healing and freedom.

Reflect, today, upon this powerful encounter this crippled man had with Jesus. Put yourself into the scene and know that this healing is also done for you. If you have not done so already this Lent, go to Confession and discover Jesus' healing in that Sacrament. Confession is the answer to the freedom that awaits you, especially when it is entered into honestly and thoroughly.

Most merciful Lord, please forgive me for my sins. I desire to see them and to acknowledge the consequences they impose upon me. I know that You desire to free me from these burdens and to heal them at the source. Lord, give me courage to confess my sins to You, especially in the Sacrament of Reconciliation. Jesus, I trust in You.

Unity with God

Wednesday of the Fourth Week of Lent

> Jesus answered the Jews: "My Father is at work until now, so I am at work." For this reason they tried all the more to kill him, because he not only broke the sabbath but he also called God his own father, making himself equal to God. John 5:17–18

Jesus was clearly guilty of grave sins in the opinion of those who sought to put Him to death. He did not follow their Sabbath laws in the way they thought He should and He revealed that He was equal to the Father. This would be a serious sin on Jesus' part if He was wrong, but obviously He wasn't.

At the heart of this passage is the unity of the Father and the Son. The verses following this passage reveal even more clearly that the Father and the Son are one and that Jesus' whole life is caught up in the fulfillment of the will of the Father. It is precisely this oneness of will that brings about their unity.

This reveals much to us about the relationship of the Father and the Son, and it also reveals much to us about our own relationship with the Father and the Son. First of all, the Father and the Son are distinct Persons, each possessing a perfect intellect and will. However, their oneness came about through the fact that their minds were in perfect harmony, knowing all things equally, and perfectly believing what they know. As a result of their perfect shared knowledge, they both embraced every detail of the plan of the Father as it was laid out from the foundation of the world.

As for us, we can take from this understanding of the unity of the Father and the Son, the glorious lesson on how we enter into unity with God. This happens first by seeking the mind of God. We must probe the glorious mysteries contained therein and must make them our own knowledge. Second, we must believe what we come to know through an act of our will. As we discover the truth, we must choose it for our lives. The challenge is that there are numerous competing voices vying for our attention. As we sort through them, choosing only that which God reveals, we naturally become attracted to the mind and will of God and make them our own. In this act, we also become one with God.

Reflect, today, upon the unity you are called to live with the Father and the Son. It is this unity that brings fulfillment to your life. It's what you were made for. Seeking, believing and embracing anything else is simply living by a lie. Seek the mind and will of God in all things and your whole being will be drawn into greater unity with God.

Father in Heaven, I thank You for the gift of Jesus Your Son and I thank You for the unity that you both share. Draw me into that glorious unity established by Your minds and wills. Make me one with You so that You also are my Father. Father in Heaven, Jesus the Son, I trust in You.

The Testimony of the Works of God

Thursday of the Fourth Week of Lent

> "The works that the Father gave me to accomplish, these works that I perform testify on my behalf that the Father has sent me." John 5:36

The *works* performed by Jesus offer *testimony* to His *mission* given Him by the Father in Heaven. Understanding this will help us to embrace our own mission in life.

First of all, let's look at the fact that Jesus' works offered *testimony*. In other words, His works spoke a message to others about who He was. The witness of His actions revealed His very essence and His union with the will of the Father.

So this begs the question, "Which works offered this testimony?" One might immediately conclude that the works Jesus was speaking of were His miracles. When people witnessed the miracles He performed they would have been convinced that He was sent from the Father in Heaven. Right? Not really. The fact of the matter is that there were many who saw Jesus perform miracles and remained stubborn, refusing to accept His miracles as proof of His divinity.

Though His miracles were extraordinary and were signs to those who were willing to believe, the most profound "work" that He performed was that of His humble and genuine love. Jesus was genuine, honest and pure of heart. He exuded every virtue one could have. Therefore, the testimony that His ordinary actions of love, care, concern and teaching gave were what would have won over many hearts first and foremost. In fact, for those who were open, His miracles were, in a sense, only icing on the cake. The "cake" was His genuine presence revealing the mercy of the Father.

You cannot perform miracles from God (unless you were given an extraordinary charism to do so), but you can act as a witness to the Truth and share the Heart of the Father in Heaven if you humbly seek to be pure of heart and allow the Heart of the Father in Heaven to shine through you in your daily actions. Even the smallest action of genuine love speaks volumes to others.

Reflect, today, upon your call to give testimony to the Father in Heaven. You are called to share the love of the Father with everyone you meet. If you embrace this mission, in great and small ways, the Gospel will be made manifest to others through you, and the will of the Father will be more fully accomplished in our world.

My genuine and holy Lord, I pray that I act as a witness to the love flowing from Your Heart. Give me the grace to be real, genuine and sincere. Help me to become a pure instrument of Your merciful Heart so that all my works will give testimony to Your mercy. Jesus, I trust in You.

The Temptation with Familiarity

Friday of the Fourth Week of Lent

> Jesus cried out in the temple area as he was teaching and said, "You know me and also know where I am from. Yet I did not come on my own, but the one who sent me, whom you do not know, is true." John 7:28

Sometimes the more familiar we are with someone the harder it is to actually see their goodness and the presence of God in their lives. Often, we are tempted to look at them and presume we "know all about them." As a result, what we can often do is simply highlight their faults and weaknesses in our minds and see them only through the lens of these faults and weaknesses.

This is what happened with Jesus. When Jesus went up to the Jewish Feast of Tabernacles, there were some there who knew Him. They probably knew Him as this ordinary son of a carpenter. Perhaps they were even from His home town. As a result of this familiarity with Jesus they immediately doubted He could be the Messiah. But they were, of course, very mistaken.

This presents a great lesson for us. It's the lesson of being judgmental and overly critical of others we know well. The more we know about someone the more we will be aware of their faults and weaknesses. And if we are not careful, we will focus in on those qualities rather than on the good qualities God wants us to see.

This is what happened with Jesus. No, He did not have any actual bad qualities. He was perfect. But there were most likely many parts of His life that invited the false judgment and criticism of others. His self-confidence, the authority He manifested in His teaching, the extraordinary compassion He had toward sinners, etc., were all exceptional qualities that some could not understand. And, as a result, they chose to be critical. "We know where He is from," they said. In other words, they did not think that someone they knew could be filled with greatness.

What do you think about those around you? What do you think about those closest to you? Are you able to see beyond any apparent weakness they have and see the hand of God at work? Are you able to see beyond the surface and see the value and dignity of their lives? When you can see the goodness of others, point it out, and be grateful for it, you will actually be seeing and loving the manifest goodness of God. God is alive and active in every soul around you. It is your responsibility to see that goodness and love it. This takes true humility on your part but, in the end, it's a way of loving God in your midst.

Reflect, today, upon how you look at those who are closest to you and spend some time trying to ponder the ways that God is alive in their lives. If you do this, you will be loving God in your very midst.

My ever-present Lord, I do love You. Help me to see and love You in others. And help me to shed any temptation I have toward being judgmental and humbly be drawn into the goodness of all Your sons and daughters. I love You, dear Lord, may I also love You in others. Jesus, I trust in You.

In Awe of Jesus
Saturday of the Fourth Week of Lent

> The guards answered, "Never before has anyone spoken like this man." John 7:46

The guards and many others were in awe of Jesus, amazed at the words He spoke. These guards were sent to arrest Jesus at the order of the chief priests and Pharisees, but the guards couldn't bring themselves to arrest Him. They were rendered powerless in the face of the "awe factor" Jesus enjoyed.

When Jesus taught, there was something communicated beyond His words. Yes, His words were powerful and transforming, but it was also the *way* in which He spoke. It was hard to explain but it's clear that, when He spoke, He also communicated a power, a calm, a conviction, and a presence. He communicated His Divine Presence and it was unmistakable. People just *knew* this man Jesus was different from all the rest and they hung on His every word.

God still communicates to us this way. Jesus still speaks to us with this "awe factor." We simply need to be attentive to it. We should strive to be attentive to the ways that God speaks in a clear and convincing way, with authority, clarity and conviction. It may be something someone says, or it may be an action of another that touches us. It may be a book we read, or a sermon we listen to. Whatever the case may be, we should look for this awe factor because it is there we will find Jesus Himself.

Interestingly, this awe factor also invited extreme criticism. Those with a simple and honest faith responded well, but those who were self-centered and self-righteous responded with condemnation and anger. They were clearly jealous. They even criticized the guards and others who were impressed by Jesus.

Reflect, today, upon the ways that God has left you in awe of His message and His love. Seek out His voice of conviction and clarity. Tune into the way God is trying to communicate and pay no attention to the ridicule and criticism you may experience when you do seek to follow His Voice. His Voice must win out and draw you in so that you can savor everything He wishes to say.

My most awe-inspiring Lord, may I be attentive to Your unmistakable Voice and to the authority with which You speak. May I be amazed at all You wish to say. And as I listen to You, dear Lord, give me the courage to respond with faith regardless of the reaction of others. I love You, dear Lord, and desire to be transfixed upon Your every Word, listening with wonder and awe. Jesus, I trust in You.

Fifth Week of Lent

Let us Go and Die With Him

Fifth Sunday of Lent (Year A)

(Note: This Gospel is also optional for Years B & C with Scrutinies)

> So Thomas, called Didymus, said to his fellow disciples, "Let us also go to die with him." John 11:16

What a great line! The context is important to understand. Thomas said this after Jesus told His Apostles that He was going up to Jerusalem because Lazarus, His friend, was ill and close to death. In fact, as the story unfolds, Lazarus actually did die before Jesus arrived at his house. Of course, we know the end of the story that Lazarus was raised up by Jesus. But the Apostles tried to keep Jesus from going to Jerusalem because they knew there were many who had been quite hostile toward Him and wanted to kill Him. But Jesus decided to go anyway. It was in this context that St. Thomas said to the others, "Let us also go and die with him." Again, what a great line!

It's a great line because Thomas appeared to say this with a certain resolve to accept whatever was waiting for them in Jerusalem. He appeared to know that Jesus was going to be met with resistance and persecution. And he also appeared to be ready to face that persecution and death with Jesus.

Of course Thomas is well known to be the doubter. After Jesus' death and Resurrection he refused to accept that the other Apostles actually saw Jesus. But even though he is well known for his act of doubting, we should not miss the courage and resolve he had in that moment. At that moment, he was willing to go with Jesus to face His persecution and death. And he was even willing to face death himself. Even though he ultimately fled when Jesus was arrested, it's believed that he eventually went as a missionary to India where he did ultimately suffer martyrdom.

This passage should help us to reflect upon our own willingness to go forth with Jesus to face any persecution that may await us. Being a Christian requires courage. We will be different than others. We will not fit in with the culture around us. And when we refuse to conform to the day and age we live in, we will most likely suffer some form of persecution as a result. Are you ready for that? Are you willing to endure this?

We also must learn from St. Thomas that, even if we do fail, we can start again. Thomas was willing, but then he fled at the sight of persecution. He ended up doubting, but in the end he courageously lived out his conviction to go and die with Jesus. It's not so much how many times we fail; rather, it's how we finish the race.

Reflect, today, upon the resolve in the heart of St. Thomas and use it as a meditation upon your own resolve. Do not worry if you fail in this resolve, you can always get up and try again. Reflect also upon the final resolution St. Thomas made when he did die a martyr. Make the choice to follow his example and you, too, will be counted among the saints in Heaven.

My resolute Lord, I desire to follow You wherever You lead. Give me a firm resolve to walk in Your ways and to imitate the courage of St. Thomas. When I fail, help me to get back up and resolve again. I love You, dear Lord, help me to love You with my life. Jesus, I trust in You.

The Call to Die

Fifth Sunday of Lent (Year B)

> "Amen, amen, I say to you, unless a grain of wheat falls to the ground and dies, it remains just a grain of wheat; but if it dies, it produces much fruit." John 12:24

Death does not necessarily sound all that inviting to most people. So, how should we look at death?

First of all, death, literally speaking, is a passing from this world to the next. When our time comes in accord with the will of God, we should welcome it and anticipate our full immersion into the life of God.

But this Scripture passage speaks of death on another level. We should see ourselves represented by the grain of wheat that achieves its potential only by falling to the ground and dying. In that natural act, it is planted in the fertile soil and grows, producing an abundance of good fruit.

How should we see ourselves represented in this natural action? We do so by embracing death to self so that we can be planted in the fertile soil of the grace of God and produce an abundance of good fruit.

Dying to oneself means that we let go of all selfishness in life. First, all intentional acts of selfishness must be let go, but then even unintended selfishness must be let go. What is "unintended selfishness?"

Unintended selfishness is a way of referring to everything in life that you hold on to and cling to simply because you want it for yourself. This could include even good things such as a loving relationship. It's not that we should do away with good things in life, such as loving relationships; rather, we must not cling to anything, even good things, for selfish motives. Love, when it is authentic love inspired by God, always is detached and selfless, looking only toward the good of the other. This is the most pure death to self that we can live. When this level of love is lived, that of complete selfless detachment, God enters into our lives and into each particular situation of our lives bringing forth an abundance of good fruit. This is a gift that is more powerful than anything we can do on our own, because it is the fruit of a total death to self, transformed by God into new life.

Reflect, today, upon your calling to die. First, reflect upon the literal death from this world that you will one day experience. Do not fear that moment; rather, see it as a glorious transition into the fullness of life. Second, look for ways that you can die to yourself, here and now. Identify practical and concrete ways that God is calling you to this form of death. Know that, in this act, glorious gifts of new life await.

My sacrificial Lord, I give myself to You and Your holy will in a total and sacrificial way. I choose to die to self so that You can bring forth new life from this act of selfless surrender. Take me, dear Lord, and do with me as You will. Jesus, I trust in You.

The Wisdom that Comes with Age

Fifth Sunday of Lent (Year C)

(Note: When the readings from Year A are used for this Sunday, the following Gospel may be used on Monday)

> "Let the one among you who is without sin be the first to throw a stone at her." Again he bent down and wrote on the ground. And in response, they went away one by one, beginning with the elders. John 8:7–9

This passage comes from the story of the woman caught in adultery when she is dragged before Jesus to see if He would support her stoning. His response is perfect and, in the end, she is left alone to encounter the tender mercy of Jesus.

Fifth Week of Lent

But there is a line in this passage that is easily overlooked. It is the line that states, "…beginning with the elders." This reveals an interesting dynamic within human communities. Generally speaking, those who are younger tend to lack the wisdom and experience that comes with age. Though the young may find it hard to admit, those who have lived a long life have a unique and broad picture of life. This enables them to be far more prudent in their decisions and judgments, especially when it comes to the more intense situations in life.

In this story, the woman is brought before Jesus with a harsh judgment. Emotions are high and these emotions clearly cloud the rational thinking of those who are ready to stone her. Jesus cuts through this irrationality by a profound statement. "Let the one among you who is without sin be the first to throw a stone at her." Perhaps, at first, those who were younger or more emotional did not allow the words of Jesus to sink in. They probably stood there with stones in hand waiting to start throwing. But then the elders began to walk away. This is age and wisdom at work. They were less controlled by the emotion of the situation and were immediately aware of the wisdom of the words spoken by our Lord. As a result, the others followed.

Reflect, today, upon the wisdom that comes with age. If you are older, reflect upon your responsibility to help guide the younger generation with clarity, firmness and love. If you are younger, do not neglect to rely upon the wisdom of the older generation. Though age is not a perfect guarantee of wisdom, it may be a far more significant factor than you realize. Be open to your elders, show them respect, and learn from the experiences they have had in life.

Prayer for the young: Lord, give me a true respect for my elders. I thank you for their wisdom stemming from the many experiences they have had in life. May I be open to their counsel and be guided by their gentle hand.

Prayer for the elder: Lord, I thank You for my life and for the many experiences I have had. I thank You for teaching me through my hardships and struggles, and I thank You for the joys and loves that I have encountered in life. Continue to pour forth Your wisdom upon me so that I may help guide Your children. May I always seek to set a good example and lead them according to Your Heart. Jesus, I trust in You.

The "Hour" of Jesus

Monday of the Fifth Week of Lent

But no one arrested him, because his hour had not yet come. John 8:20

This short line comes at the end of today's Gospel after Jesus, once again, directly confronted the Pharisees. He confronts them, in this situation, by speaking the truth of His union with the Father and the power and authority He had on account of this union. The Pharisees attempt to confront and challenge Him but He speaks the truth right back to them in clear language. Their response to Jesus' words is not recorded but it's clear that they do not know what to say and it's clear that they remain skeptical and desirous of trapping Jesus.

This passage quoted above reveals to us the profound truth that neither the malice of the Pharisees nor that of anyone else could ultimately triumph since Jesus' "hour had not yet come." What does this mean? Here are two truths we should take from this line.

First, malice cannot overpower the will of God. Since God the Father did not permit Jesus' arrest at that time, those with evil intentions were powerless to do so. Jesus was able to speak clearly and openly, challenging the Pharisees with the truth, and they could do nothing to stop it. Though His words stung them to the heart, they could do no more than listen and grow in anger and obstinacy toward our Lord. But they could not harm Him. This shows that God is ultimately in control of even the malice of others and will only allow malice to appear to triumph when He sees some greater purpose for allowing such a thing to happen.

Secondly, it reveals that there is a coming "hour" when Jesus will be handed over to sinful men. But in John's Gospel, this hour is not an hour of shame and disgrace for Jesus; rather, it is an hour of total triumph over sin and death. From a worldly perspective we know that His hour of arrest, persecution and Crucifixion takes on the public appearance of horror and disgrace for Jesus. It appears as if He lost and the Pharisees won. But from the perspective of God, which is the only true perspective, Jesus triumphs gloriously. In fact, the Father ultimately permits the malice of the Pharisees to be the instrument of Jesus' glorification through the sufferings He endured in this hour. From the divine perspective, His hour does not become one of defeat; rather, it becomes one of ultimate victory.

Reflect, today, upon the coming hour of Jesus. Soon we will enter into the glories of Holy Week and ponder, once again, that the Father did permit Jesus to enter into the most cruel suffering and death imaginable. We will be confronted with the apparent scandal of His arrest and the illusion of the victory of the malicious leaders of the day. But their victory is only an illusion since the permissive will of the Father had other intentions. Begin preparing for this annual celebration of the hour of Jesus and enter into it with the utmost confidence and faith.

My glorious Lord, I glorify You for Your wisdom and power and rejoice in the perfect will of the Father in Heaven. The Father sent You on a mission of redemption and salvation and permitted You to ultimately suffer and die. But through this suffering He brought final victory over death and all evil. Give me faith to know and believe this truth with my whole heart. Bless this coming Holy Week, dear Lord, and permit me to rejoice in Your glorious victory. Jesus, I trust in You.

The Abiding Presence of God

Tuesday of the Fifth Week of Lent

> "The one who sent me is with me. He has not left me alone." John 8:29

Most young children, if left at home all alone, would react with fear. They need to know that their parents are around. The idea of being somewhere all by themselves is frightening. It would be just as frightening for a child to get lost in a store or another public place. They need the security that comes with a parent being near.

The same is true in the spiritual life. Interiorly, if we sense we are all alone we may react with fear. To feel as though there is an interior abandonment from God is a frightening thought. But on the contrary, when we sense that God is very present and alive within us, we are greatly strengthened to face life with courage and joy.

This was Jesus' experience in the passage above in which He speaks much about His relationship with the Father. The Father is the One who sent Jesus into the world for His mission and Jesus acknowledges that the Father will not leave Him alone. Jesus says this, knows it and experiences the blessing of that relationship in His human and divine Heart.

The same can be said of each one of us. First, we must come to realize that the Father has sent us. We each have a mission in life. Do you realize that? Do you realize that you have a very specific mission and calling from God? Yes, it may entail very ordinary parts of life such as chores around the house, the daily grind of work, the building up of your family relationships, etc. Our daily lives are filled with ordinary activities that make up the will of God.

It may be possible that you are already fully immersed in the will of God for your life. But it is also possible that God wants more from you. He has a plan for you and it's a mission that He has not entrusted to another. It may require that you step out in faith, be courageous, move out of your comfort zone, or face some fear. But whatever the case may be, God has a mission for you.

The comforting news is that God does not just send us, He also remains with us. He has not left us alone to fulfill the mission He has entrusted to us. He has promised His continued help in a very central way.

Reflect, today, about the mission that Jesus was given: the mission to give His life in a sacrificial way. Also reflect upon how God wants you to live out this same mission with Christ of sacrificial love and self-giving. You may already be living it wholeheartedly, or you may need some new direction. Say "Yes" to it with courage and confidence and God will walk with you every step of the way.

My sacrificial Lord, I say "Yes" to the perfect plan you have for my life. Whatever it may be I accept without hesitation, dear Lord. I know that You are always with me and that I am never alone. Jesus, I trust in You.

Freedom From Sin

Wednesday of the Fifth Week of Lent

> Jesus answered them, "Amen, amen, I say to you, everyone who commits sin is a slave of sin. A slave does not remain in a household forever, but a son always remains. So if the Son frees you, then you will truly be free." John 8:34–36

Jesus wants to set you free, but do you want to be set free? On an intellectual level this should be an easy question to answer. Of course you want your freedom! Who wouldn't? But on a practical level this question is harder to answer. Practically speaking, many people are very comfortable living in sin. Sin offers a deceptive satisfaction that can be hard to turn away from. Sin can make you "feel" good in the moment, even though the long-term effects are that it strips your freedom and joy. But so often that momentary "satisfaction" is enough for many people to keep coming back.

So what about you? Do you want to be free so as to live as a son or daughter of the Most High God? If you answer "Yes" then be prepared for this to be painful, but in a delightful way. Overcoming sin requires purification. The process of "letting go" of sin requires true sacrifice and commitment. It requires you to turn to the Lord in absolute trust and abandon. In doing so, you experience a sort of death to yourself, to your passions and to your own selfish will. This hurts, at least on the level of your fallen human nature. But it's like a surgery that has the goal of removing cancer or some infection. The surgery itself may hurt, but it's the only way to be freed of the malady you have. The Son is the Divine Surgeon and the way He sets you free is through His own suffering and death. Jesus' Crucifixion and death brought life into the world. His death destroyed the disease of sin, and our willing acceptance of the remedy of His death means we must let Him destroy the disease of sin within us through His death. It must be "cut out" so to speak and removed by our Lord.

Lent is a time, more than any, in which you must honestly focus on your sin for the reason of identifying those things that keep you bound, so that you can invite the Divine Physician to enter your wounds and heal you. Do not let Lent go by without honestly examining your conscience thoroughly, and repenting of your sins with all your heart. The Lord wants you to be free! Desire it yourself and enter the process of purification so that you will be relieved of your heavy burdens.

Reflect, today, upon your attitude toward your own personal sins. First, can you humbly admit to your sin? Don't rationalize them away or blame another. Face them and accept them as your own. Second, confess your sins. Reflect upon your attitude toward the Sacrament of Reconciliation. This is the Sacrament of freedom. It is so very easy. Just go in, admit all your sins, express sorrow and be set free. If you find this difficult then you are trusting your own feelings of fear rather than the truth. Third, rejoice in the freedom that the Son of God offers you. It's a gift beyond anything we deserve. Reflect on these three things today and for the rest of Lent, and your Easter will be one of true thanksgiving!

Lord, I do desire to be set free from all sin so that I may live in the freedom of being Your child. Help me, dear Lord, to face my sin with honesty and openness. Give me the courage I need to admit my sin in the Sacrament of Reconciliation, so that I may rejoice in all that You have bestowed upon me through Your suffering and death. Jesus, I trust in You.

The Power of Destructive Speech

Thursday of the Fifth Week of Lent

> Jesus said to the Jews: "Amen, amen, I say to you, whoever keeps my word will never see death." So the Jews said to him, "Now we are sure that you are possessed." John 8:51–52

It's hard to imagine anything worse that could be said about Jesus. Did they really think He was possessed by the evil one? It appears so. What a sad and bizarre thing to say about the Son of God. Here is God Himself, in the person of Jesus, offering a promise of eternal life. He reveals the sacred Truth that obedience to His Word is the pathway to eternal happiness and that everyone needs to know this Truth and live it. Jesus speaks this freely and openly, but the response from some hearing this message is deeply disappointing, slanderous and malicious.

It's hard to know what was going on in their minds to cause them to say such a thing. Perhaps they were jealous of Jesus, or perhaps they were just seriously confused. Whatever the case may be, they spoke something that was seriously damaging.

The damage of such a statement was not so much toward Jesus; rather, it was damaging to themselves as well as to those around Him. Jesus could personally handle whatever was spoken about Him, but others could not. It is important to understand that our own words can do great damage to ourselves and to others.

First of all, their words did damage to themselves. By speaking such an erroneous statement <u>publicly</u>, they start down the path of obstinacy. It takes great humility to retract such a statement in the future. So it is with us. When we verbalize something that is damaging toward another, it's hard to retract it. It's hard to later apologize and mend the wound we have caused. The damage is primarily done to our own heart in that it's hard to let go of our error and humbly move forward. But this must be done if we want to undo the damage.

Secondly, this comment also did damage to those who were listening. Some may have rejected this malicious statement but others may have pondered it and started to wonder if in fact Jesus was possessed. Thus, seeds of doubt were sown. We must all realize that our words affect others and we must strive to speak them with the utmost care and charity.

Reflect, today, upon your own speech. Are there things you have spoken to others that you now realize were erroneous or misleading? If so, have you sought to undo the damage by retracting your words and apologizing? Reflect, also, upon the fact that it's easy to be drawn into the malicious conversation of others. Have you allowed yourself to be influenced by such conversations? If so, resolve to silence your ears to such errors and look for ways to speak the truth.

Lord of all Truth, give me the grace of speaking holy words that always give You glory and reflect the eternal Truths alive in Your Heart. Help me to also be aware of the lies all around me in this world of sin. May Your Heart filter out the errors and allow only the seeds of Truth to be planted in my own mind and heart. Jesus, I trust in You.

The Crucifixion Draws Near

Friday of the Fifth Week of Lent

> The Jews picked up rocks to stone Jesus. Jesus answered them, "I have shown you many good works from my Father. For which of these are you trying to stone me?" John 10:31–32

As we draw closer to Holy Week, and to Good Friday, we begin to see that hatred was growing toward Jesus. Just as we saw in yesterday's reflection, this makes no sense. To hate Jesus and to desire to stone Him to death is an act of the greatest irrationality. But this is what happened. Little by little, those who were against Jesus grew in boldness until that ultimate day came when He laid down His life for us and willingly embraced His death.

Over the next two weeks it's good to face this irrationality and persecution head on. It's good to see the hatred of so many and to name it for what it is. No, it's not a pleasant thought, but it is reality. It's the world we live in. And it's a reality we will all face in our lives.

When confronting evil and persecution, we should do so as Jesus did. He faced it without fear. He faced it with the truth and never accepted the lies and calumny that so many threw at Him.

The fact of the matter is that the closer we grow toward God, the greater the persecution and hatred we will encounter. Again, this may not make sense to us. It's easy to think that if we are close to God and strive for holiness everyone will love and praise us. But it wasn't that way for Jesus and it will not be that way for us either.

One key to holiness is that in the midst of persecution, suffering, hardship and sorrow, we stand firm in the truth. It's always tempting to think that we must be doing something wrong when things do not go our way. It's easy to be confused by the lies and calumny that the world throws at us when we try to stand for goodness and the truth. One thing God wants of us, in the midst of our own crosses, is to purify our faith and resolve to stand firm in His Word and Truth.

When we face some cross or some persecution it can be like getting hit in the head. We may feel like we are in a daze and can give into panic and fear. But these are the times, more than any other, when we need to stand strong. We need to remain humble but deeply convicted about all that God has said and revealed to us. This deepens our ability to trust God in all things. It's easy to say we trust God when life is easy, it's hard to trust Him when the cross we face is quite heavy.

Reflect, today, upon the fact that no matter what your cross may be, it is a gift from God in that He is desiring to strengthen you for some greater purpose. As Saint John Paul the Great said over and over during his pontificate,

"Do not be afraid!" Face your fears and let God transform you in the midst of them. If you do so, you will discover that your greatest struggles in life actually turn out to be your greatest blessings.

My courageous Lord, as we draw near to the commemoration of Your own suffering and death, help me to unite my crosses to Yours. Help me to see in my daily struggle Your presence and strength. Help me to see the purpose you have for me in the midst of these challenges. Jesus, I trust in You.

One Man Should Die

Saturday of the Fifth Week of Lent

> But one of them, Caiaphas, who was high priest that year, said to them, "You know nothing, nor do you consider that it is better for you that one man should die instead of the people, so that the whole nation may not perish." John 11:49–50

As in the previous day's reflection, it's important for us to start putting our focus on the suffering and death of Jesus. Holy Week begins this Sunday, so this is the time of year when God wants us to look intently at His Cross. It's important to look at it from all angles, to try to understand what was going on, what Jesus was experiencing, what the disciples were experiencing and even what the Pharisees and high priests were experiencing.

In today's Gospel quoted above, we see the thinking of Caiaphas, the high priest. His words are interesting in that they are both sad and prophetic at the same time. He, along with the other chief priests and the Pharisees, were beginning to plan and plot Jesus' death. But what's insightful is the apparent motivation of Caiaphas and the others.

Jesus was gaining popularity and they were afraid that this popularity would stir things up with the Romans. They were also jealous that Jesus had attracted so many. So Caiaphas offers the twisted logic that it's better that one man die rather than all of the people. In other words, he appeared to think that because Jesus was becoming so popular, and the people were listening to Jesus more than they were to the chief priests and Pharisees, that it was better to eliminate the "problem" so that things could return to the way they were.

This reveals the fact that the Pharisees were more concerned about themselves and their status than they were about the Truth. It's amazing that one of their criticisms of Jesus was that He was doing too many signs and wonders. How strange. If the chief priests and Pharisees were interested in the Truth, they would have also seen the glory and divine authority of Jesus and come to believe in Him and follow Him. But they couldn't swallow their pride and accept the call to follow someone other than themselves. They couldn't let go of their position of authority.

We often see this same experience in our daily lives. We want to be the center of attention. And so often when we see someone else do well or receive praise we can get jealous. And our jealousy can often turn into a form of envy. Envy means we are angered and saddened by the goodness of another. We can brew over it and want to see them fail.

The ideal is to be one of those faithful followers of Jesus. This is especially important to ponder this coming week as you witness the hostility grow toward our Lord. What would you do if you were there? Would you continue to stand with Jesus despite the attacks of others? As the hostility toward Jesus grew, would you back away from Him or grow closer to Him in love and commitment?

Reflect, today, upon the coming commemoration of the persecution of our Lord. Let your mind begin to ponder the many reactions and experiences people had that first Holy Week. Put yourself in their shoes and try to live it with Jesus. The goal is to find ourselves there at the foot of the Cross with Him on Good Friday with love and courage, standing by Him and loving Him every step of the way.

My persecuted Lord, may I follow You this coming Holy Week. May I have the love I need to love You even in Your rejection and pain. Help me to shed all envy and selfishness and to see You especially in the sufferings of others and in their goodness. Jesus, I trust in You.

Holy Week

Let it Begin...

Palm Sunday of the Lord's Passion (Year A)

> And when he entered Jerusalem the whole city was shaken and asked, "Who is this?" And the crowds replied, "This is Jesus the prophet, from Nazareth in Galilee." Matthew 21:10–11

As Jesus entered Jerusalem, just four short days before He would be arrested, He was received with great joy. As He entered, riding a donkey, the crowds spread their cloaks, strewed palm branches before Him and cried out, "Hosanna to the Son of David; blessed is he who comes in the name of the Lord; hosanna in the highest" (Mt. 21:9). Jesus was the King of Kings and Lord of Lords, and He was given a Kingly welcome.

Jerusalem itself was the place of the Temple where so many of the ancient kings of Israel offered sacrifice to God. Year after year, decade after decade, and century after century, the high priest entered the Holy of Holies within the Temple to offer sacrifice to God. However, little did anyone know that as Jesus entered Jerusalem, the entire city became the new Temple and Jesus became the final and definitive Priest. He entered this new Holy of Holies as a King and Priest, and He died as the Sacrificial Lamb. He was greeted with shouts of "Hosanna" only to soon hear "Crucify Him, crucify Him!"

What a turn of emotions. What a contrast of experiences. What a shock to the minds and hearts of all of His first followers. How could this be? How could something so glorious become so painful in such a short amount of time? From an earthly perspective, what would soon follow made no sense, but from a divine perspective, it was the beginning of the most glorious act ever known.

The evil one certainly watched in hatred and jealousy as Jesus, the Eternal Son of the Father, was given this glorious reception by these sons and daughters of God. The envy of the evil one was so great that it became alive and manifest in the souls of some of the religious leaders, in the betrayal of one of the Apostles, in the actions of the civil authorities and in the confused emotions of the crowds. The vile, frightful, forceful and definitive attack on our Lord would soon begin now that He was welcomed into the city of Jerusalem to begin the Feast of Passover. Who could have known that on that Passover the Lamb of Sacrifice would be our Lord Himself.

In our own lives, we often do all we can to avoid even the slightest amount of sacrifice. But sacrifice is capable of the greatest good when united to the one Sacrifice of Jesus. Jesus entered Jerusalem with perfect determination to begin the Sacrifice that would conquer sin and death and defeat the evil one. And that is exactly what He did.

Reflect, today, upon how willing you are to embrace sacrifice in your own life. No, your sacrifices are not able to save the world by their own merit, but if you face your crosses in life, be they big or small, and if you intentionally and wholeheartedly unite them to the actions of Jesus that first Holy Week, then you can be certain that you will suffer with our Lord. But you can also be certain that your suffering will be transformed by the power of this Holy Week and lead you to a glorious sharing in His triumph over all sin and suffering. Sacrifice yourself with our Lord this Holy Week so that you, too, will rise victorious with our Lord.

My glorious Lord, I cry out to You, "Hosanna!" You are the King, the High Priest, and the Spotless Lamb of Sacrifice. As I enter into this Holy Week, enable me to walk with You and to offer my own life as a sacrifice in union with Your own perfect Sacrifice. May Your

Holy Week transcend time and permeate every aspect of my life so that, as I die with You, I may also share in the glory of Your Resurrection. Jesus, I trust in You.

From Glory to Glory

Palm Sunday of the Lord's Passion (Year B)

> Those preceding him as well as those following kept crying out: "Hosanna! Blessed is he who comes in the name of the Lord! Blessed is the kingdom of our father David that is to come! Hosanna in the highest!" Mark 11:9–10

As Jesus entered Jerusalem at the beginning of the first Holy Week, He was welcomed with much enthusiasm, and He accepted the love and devotion of those who welcomed Him. He was their King. He was the Messiah, and the welcome they gave to Him was but a pale gift of the true adoration He deserved. And though Jesus entered Jerusalem with this glorious welcome, less than a week later He would leave Jerusalem with a heavy cross on His shoulders, carrying it outside the city walls to die.

When we contrast the entry of Jesus on Palm Sunday with His arrest, abuse, mock trial, carrying of the cross and death, these two extremes do appear to be at the opposite ends of the spectrum. There is rejoicing and praise as He enters, and sorrow and shock as He leaves. But are these two events all that different from a divine perspective? From the perspective of the Father in Heaven, the end of the week is nothing other than the ultimate culmination of the full glory of His Son.

Today we read the long and beautiful account of the Passion of Jesus as told in Mark's Gospel. But on Friday we will read the account of John's Gospel. Mark's Gospel tells the story in clear detail, but John's Gospel will most notably add the spiritual insight that Jesus' crucifixion and death is nothing other than His hour of glory. We will see His Cross as His new throne of grace, and the earthly glory Jesus receives today as He enters Jerusalem will be fully realized from a divine perspective as He mounts His Throne of the Cross to take up His eternal Kingship.

As we enter into the holiest week of the year, it is essential that each of us see the journey of Christ this week as our own calling in life. We must journey toward the glory of the Cross with our Lord. From a worldly perspective, the Cross does not make sense. But from the perspective of the Father in Heaven, the Cross is not only the source of the greatest glory of His Son, but it is also the path by which we share in that glory. We must die with Him, sacrifice all for Him, choose to follow Him, and hold nothing back in our resolve to lay down our lives out of love.

Reflect, today, upon the events you will commemorate this week. Commit yourself to share in them, not just as an intellectual remembrance but as a living participation. How is God calling You to step forward in a sacrificial way out of love? How is God calling you to courageously embrace your calling to give your life away? Strive to see this week from the perspective of the Father in Heaven and pray that you will also see the ways in which the Father is calling you to imitate His Son. Let us go and die with Him, for it is in the Cross of Christ that we will discover His eternal glory.

My glorious King, You are worthy of all praise and adoration. Hosanna to You, hosanna in the highest! Draw me into Your glorious passion, dear Lord, and help me to see the glory of Your Cross. As I see its glory, give me the grace I need to share more fully in Your life of transforming sacrificial love. Jesus, I trust in You.

A Shocking Contrast!
Palm Sunday of the Lord's Passion (Year C)

> "Blessed is the king who comes in the name of the Lord. Peace in heaven and glory in the highest." Luke 19:38

In today's Liturgy, we face quite a contrast of experiences and emotions. We begin our celebration listening to the story of Jesus being welcomed into Jerusalem with great joy and exultation! "Hosanna!" they cried out. "Hosanna in the Highest!" Jesus was treated as He should have been treated. People were excited to see Him and there was much excitement.

But this excitement quickly turned to shock and horror as we enter more deeply into today's readings. The Gospel culminates with Jesus hanging on the Cross crying out "Eloi, Eloi, lema sabachthani?" "My God, my God, why have you forsaken me?" And with that, "Jesus gave a loud cry and breathed his last." At that moment the entire congregation kneels in silence as we ponder the reality of Christ's death.

How things can change in one short week. What happened to all the people who were shouting and praising Him as He entered into Jerusalem? How could they allow Him to enter into this Crucifixion and death?

The deepest answer to this question is one that we may not expect. The answer is that the Father willed it. The Father willed, by His permissive will, that so many would turn on Him, abandon Him and allow Him to be crucified. This is so very important to understand.

At any time during that first Holy Week, Jesus could have exercised His divine power and refused to embrace His Cross. But He didn't. Instead, He willingly walked through this week anticipating and embracing the suffering and rejection He received. And He didn't do so begrudgingly or even with regret. He embraced this week willingly, choosing it as His own will.

Why would He do such a thing? Why would He choose suffering and death? Because in the Father's perfect wisdom, this suffering and death was for a greater purpose. God chose to confound the wisdom of the world by using His own suffering and Crucifixion as the perfect means of our holiness. In this act, He transformed the greatest evil into the greatest good. Now, as a result of our faith in this act, the crucifix hangs centrally in our churches and in our homes as a constant reminder that not even the greatest of evils can overcome the power, wisdom and love of God. God is more powerful than death itself and God has the final victory even when all seems lost.

Let this week give you divine hope. So often we can be tempted toward discouragement and, even worse, we can be tempted toward despair. But all is not lost for us either. Nothing can ultimately steal away our joy unless we let it. No hardship, no burden and no cross can conquer us if we remain steadfast in Christ Jesus letting Him transform all we endure in life by His glorious embrace of His own Cross.

Reflect, today, upon the contrast of emotions from Palm Sunday through Good Friday. Ponder the fear, confusion and despair that many would have had as they saw Jesus murdered. Reflect, also, upon this being a divine act by which the Father permitted this grave suffering so as to use it for the greatest good ever known. The Lord gave His life freely and calls you to do the same. Reflect upon the cross in your life. Know that the Lord can use this for good, bringing forth an abundance of mercy through your free embrace as you offer it to Him as a willing sacrifice. Blessed Holy Week! Put your eyes upon the Lord's Cross as well as your own.

My crucified Lord, when I am tempted to despair, give me hope. Help me to see your presence in all things, even in those things that are most troubling to me. May this Holy Week transform my darkest moments and weakness as I surrender all to You, my God. Jesus, I trust in You.

Anointing the Feet of Jesus
Monday of Holy Week

> Mary took a liter of costly perfumed oil made from genuine aromatic nard and anointed the feet of Jesus and dried them with her hair; the house was filled with the fragrance of the oil. John 12:3

What a humble and beautiful act of love toward Jesus. This perfume was worth 300 days' wages. That's a lot of money! It's interesting to note that Judas objected to this act by claiming that he thought it should have been sold and the money given to the poor. But the Gospel states clearly that Judas was really only interested in the money himself since he used to steal from the money bag. Of even greater note is Jesus' response to Judas. Jesus rebukes Judas and states, "Leave her alone. Let her keep this for the day of my burial. You always have the poor with you, but you do not always have me."

If anyone else would have said this it would have sounded self-centered. But it was Jesus who said it and He was perfectly selfless in His love. So what was this all about? It was about the fact that Jesus knew what Mary needed. And in saying what He did, He revealed what each one of us needs. We need to worship Him, honor Him and make Him the center of our lives. We need to humble ourselves before Him and serve Him. Not because He needs us to treat Him this way, but because we need to treat Him this way. Honoring Him in our humility and love is what we need to do for our own holiness and happiness. Jesus knew this, so He honored Mary for this act of love.

This story invites us to do the same. It invites us to look to Jesus and to make Him the center of our adoration and love. It invites us to willingly pour out all our labor for Him (symbolized by the perfume worth 300 days' wages). Nothing is too costly for Jesus. Nothing is worth more than an act of our worship.

Worship of God is right to do. Most importantly, it's an act that will transform you into the person you were made to be. You were made for worship and adoration of God and this is accomplished when you humbly honor our Lord with your whole self.

Reflect, today, upon the depth of your own adoration of our Lord. Are you willing to "spill" your whole livelihood upon Him? Is He worth more to you than 300 days' wages? Is He the most central part of your life? Do you daily humble yourself before Him and pour out your heart to Him in prayer? Reflect upon this humble act of worship that Mary offers Jesus and seek to imitate her beautiful example.

Lord, may I follow the example of this holy woman, Mary. Help me to humble myself before You and honor You with my whole life. Dear Lord, nothing in life is more important than You and my total adoration of You. Draw me in, dear Lord, humble me before Your glory and help me to love and worship You with my whole being. Jesus, I trust in You.

Painful Betrayal

Tuesday of Holy Week

> Reclining at table with his disciples, Jesus was deeply troubled and testified, "Amen, amen, I say to you, one of you will betray me." John 13:21

It's very important to note here that Jesus was "deeply troubled." This shows His humanity. Jesus had a human heart and loved Judas with a divine love through His human heart. As a result of this perfect love of Judas, Jesus' heart was deeply troubled. It was "troubled" in the sense that Jesus could do nothing more than He had already done to change the mind and heart of Judas. It's not that Jesus was personally offended or angered by Judas' betrayal. Rather, it's that Jesus' heart burned with a deep sorrow at the loss of Judas whom He loved with a perfect love.

Judas had free will. Without free will Judas could not freely love Jesus. But with free will, Judas chose to betray Jesus. The same is true with us. We have free will and we are given the same ability that Judas had to accept the love of Jesus or to reject it. We can let His loving gift of salvation and grace enter our lives or refuse it. It's 100% up to us.

Holy Week is an ideal time to seriously contemplate the road you are on. Each and every day of your life you are invited by God to choose Him with all your might and love. But, like Judas, we so often betray Him by our refusal to enter Holy Week with Jesus, embracing His Cross as ours. We so often fail to give completely of our lives in a sacrificial and generous way, as our Lord did that Holy Week.

Reflect, today, upon the love Jesus had for Judas. It was His love for Judas, more than Judas' sin, that brought so much pain to Jesus' Heart. If Jesus didn't love him, the rejection would not have hurt. Reflect, also, on the love Jesus has for you. Ponder whether or not His Heart is also troubled as a result of the actions in your life. Be honest and do not make excuses. If Jesus is troubled in any way as a result of your actions and choices this is no reason to despair as Judas did. Rather, it should be the cause of rejoicing that you are aware of your weakness, sin and limitation. Turn that over to Jesus who loves you more than you love yourself. Doing this will bring your heart much consolation and peace. And it will also bring much consolation and peace to the Heart of our Divine Lord. He loves you and is waiting for you to come to Him this Holy Week.

My dear suffering and rejected Lord, I do love You but I also know that I cause Your Heart to be troubled by my betrayal. Help me to see my sin honestly this Holy Week. In seeing it, may I let go of that which keeps me from loving You more deeply, so as to walk with You to the Cross to share in Your glorious triumph. Jesus, I trust in You.

Stuck in Denial

Wednesday of Holy Week

> The Son of Man indeed goes, as it is written of him, but woe to that man by whom the Son of Man is betrayed. It would be better for that man if he had never been born." Then Judas, his betrayer, said in reply, "Surely it is not I, Rabbi?" He answered, "You have said so." Matthew 26:24–25

Was Judas in denial? Did he truly think that he was not the one who was to betray Jesus? We do not know for certain what was going on in Judas' mind, but one thing is clear...he did betray Jesus. And it appears from his words that he didn't see his act as a betrayal and, therefore, he was in deep denial.

Denial, if written out as an acronym, has been said to mean that I "don't even know I am lying." Perhaps Judas was so steeped in his own sin that he couldn't even admit to himself, let alone to others, that he was lying and preparing to betray Jesus for money. This is a scary thought.

It's scary because it reveals one of the effects of persistent sin. Persistent sin makes sin easier. And eventually, when one persists in the same sin, that sin is easily rationalized, justified and denied as sin altogether. When one gets stuck in this downward spiral of persistent sin it's hard to get out. And often the only way to survive the psychological tension is to remain in denial.

This is an important lesson for us this Holy Week. Sin is never fun to look at and takes great courage to do so. But imagine if Judas would have actually confessed to what he was about to do. Imagine if he would have broken down in front of Jesus and the other Apostles and told them the whole truth. Perhaps that act of honesty would have saved his life and his eternal soul. It would have been painful and humiliating for him to do so, but it would have been the right thing to do.

The same is true with you. Perhaps you are not at a point where your sin is leading you to outright betrayal of Jesus, but everyone can find some pattern of sin in their lives this Holy Week. You must seek to discover, with God's help, some pattern or habit you have formed. What a great discovery this would be if you could then face this sin with honesty and courage. This would enable you to shed any bit of denial regarding your sin and enable you to conquer that sin so as to discover the freedom God wants you to experience!

Reflect, today, upon Judas saying to Jesus, "Surely it is not I, Rabbi?" This sad statement from Judas must have deeply wounded our Lord's Heart as He witnessed the denial of Judas. Reflect, also, upon the many times that you deny your sin, failing to sincerely repent. Make this Holy Week a time for honesty and integrity. The Lord's mercy is so deep and pure that, if you would understand it, you would have no need to remain in any form of denial of your sins.

Lord, help me this Holy Week to have the courage I need to face my sin and weakness. I am a sinner, dear Lord, but it can be very hard for me to admit it. May I entrust my sin to You so that I may be set free and receive, in its place, Your abundant mercy. Jesus, I trust in You.

Cleansed by the Greatest Humility
Holy Thursday, Mass of the Lord's Supper (Reflection One)

> Peter said to him, "You will never wash my feet." Jesus answered him, "Unless I wash you, you will have no inheritance with me." John 13:8

It was a beautiful image of the deepest humility ever witnessed. Jesus, the Eternal Son of God, the Second Person of the Most Holy Trinity, was exercising the duty of a servant. One by one, Jesus went around and cleansed the feet of His disciples. It was the celebration of the Passover. A holy feast, a remembrance of God's saving action to their ancestors the night they were set free from slavery in Egypt. However, this Passover "remembrance" was certainly one to be remembered, and embraced.

Peter was overwhelmed by Jesus' humility and at first refused to have his Lord wash his feet. But Jesus says something that rings true for all eternity: "Unless I wash you, you will have no inheritance with me." This was no ordinary washing, it was not in reference only to the washing of Peter's dirty feet, it was an eternal washing of his immortal soul, and the "water" would soon flow forth from the pierced and Sacred Heart of Jesus Himself.

Less than twenty-four hours later, Jesus would be on a cross, and a Roman soldier would pierce His heart with a lance. From His heart flowed blood and water, the new font of grace and mercy itself. This "Last Supper" with our Lord was the sacramental institution of the cleansing power of His one and perfect Sacrifice which is now made present to us throughout time in the gifts of Baptism, Confirmation and the Holy Eucharist.

Every time we renew our Baptism, receive His Spirit more deeply into our lives and consume His sacred Body and Blood, we participate in this cleansing action of Christ to Peter and the other disciples. Jesus looks at each one of us, with a gaze of love, and says, "Unless I wash you…" What is your response to our Lord?

It takes humility to accept the humblest act of mercy ever known. We must humbly acknowledge that we need our Lord to cleanse us, to wipe the dirt from our souls, to redeem us and to offer us the inheritance of everlasting life.

It is at that Last Supper, the beginning of the first Triduum of Holy Thursday, Good Friday and Easter Sunday, that our Lord gazes through Peter to each one of us and offers to cleanse us of all sin. What is your response? How humble are you in your reception of this gift? How deeply do you believe in the saving Sacrifice of our divine Lord?

Reflect, this night, upon those sacred words of our Lord and hear them spoken to you: "Unless I wash you, you will have no inheritance with me." Say "Yes" to this offer of perfect humility and mercy from our Lord and let the saving Sacrifice of the Son of God enter more deeply into your life than ever before.

My merciful Lord, Your humility is awe-inspiring and overwhelming. Please wash me clean with the blood and water flowing forth from Your pierced Heart. Help me to receive this gift in the way it was given: with humility. I thank You, I say "Yes" to Your gift, I receive You and I invite You to cleanse me. I am a sinner, dear Lord. I need Your cleansing action in my life. Jesus, I trust in You.

Humility of Service, Nourished by the Eucharist

Holy Thursday, Mass of the Lord's Supper (Reflection Two)

"This is my body that is for you. Do this in remembrance of me." 1 Cor. 11:24

We begin, today, the Triduum—the three great celebrations of our Catholic Faith. Yes, there are numerous celebrations that take place throughout the year. But these three celebrations are the heart of our faith and are the culmination of all of our worship. We begin today with the celebration of the Lord's gift of the Most Holy Eucharist given through the priesthood He instituted. Tomorrow we enter into the mystery of His Crucifixion. Saturday after sundown we enter into the glory of His Resurrection.

On Holy Thursday evening, we begin the Triduum with the commemoration of the Last Supper. This event in history, which took place as a Passover meal shared with Jesus and His Apostles, begins the gift that brings us salvation.

On Holy Thursday, we hear the Lord say for the first time, "This is my body that is for you." We hear Him point to the gift of the Holy Eucharist as His gift to us, given for our holiness and fulfillment. It's a gift we will never be able to fathom or comprehend. It's the gift of His complete self-giving and sacrificial love.

If we could only understand the Eucharist! If we could only understand this precious and sacred gift! The Eucharist is God Himself, present in our world, and given to us to transform us into that which we consume. The Eucharist, in a real way, transforms us into Christ Himself. As we consume the Holy Eucharist, we are drawn into the divine life of the Most Holy Trinity. We are made one with God and are given the food of eternity.

On that first Holy Thursday, Jesus also offered an example of the perfect humility and service that we are called to imitate as we become one with Him. He washed the feet of His Apostles so as to teach them and us that His Body and Blood are given so as to enable us to love as He loved. The Eucharist transforms us into true servants who are called to humility. We are called to humble service of others. This service will take on various forms but it is what we are called to.

Do you serve those around you? Do you humble yourself before others to care for their most basic needs? Do you show them you love them by your actions? This is at the heart of Holy Thursday. Humble service is a beautiful expression of our own intimate union with the Son of God.

So often, true "greatness" is misunderstood. Greatness is often perceived with a secular understanding of success and admiration. Too often we want others to admire our accomplishments. But Jesus offers another view of greatness. On Holy Thursday, He shows that true greatness is found in this humble act of service. Imitating Him requires that we surrender our pride. And this is made possible when we consume the Holy Eucharist with faith. The Eucharist enables us to love and serve others in this humble way. And that love and service is an act that will win the hearts and souls of others for the Kingdom of God.

As we celebrate Holy Thursday, we are all challenged to ponder our humility and to commit ourselves to a radical and total gift of self to others.

Reflect, this night, upon whether or not you imitate the humility of our Lord. Are you committed to seeking ways in which you can serve others, showing them you love and care for them? Let Holy Thursday transform you so that you can imitate the great love that Jesus offered us on this glorious night.

My humble Lord, help me to understand what it means to be a servant. Help me to live this humility in my actions. May the gift of Your most

Sacred Body and Blood transform me into the person You desire me to be. Jesus, I trust in You.

God Suffers Human Death
Good Friday of the Lord's Passion (Reflection One)

Ponder today, this dark day, the final words of Jesus. Scripture records seven last statements, or the "Seven Last Words." Take each phrase and spend time with it. Seek the deeper spiritual meaning for your life.

"Father, forgive them, for they know not what they do."

Jesus' forgiveness of others was radical and to a degree never seen before. While hanging on the Cross and enduring the cruelty of others, Jesus spoke words of forgiveness. He forgave them in the midst of His persecution.

What's more is that He even acknowledged that those crucifying Him were not fully responsible. They clearly did not know what they were doing. This humble acknowledgment of Jesus shows the depth of His tender mercy. It reveals He died not in anger or resentment, but in willing sacrifice.

Can you say these words? Can you call to mind the person who has hurt you and pray that the Father forgives them? Leave judgment to God and offer mercy and forgiveness.

"I assure you, today you will be with me in paradise."

What a consolation it must have been for the good thief to hear these words. He must have been experiencing a certain despair in life at that moment as he, along side of Jesus, was dying on a cross. What a gift it was to be there next to the Savior of the World, sharing in the sufferings of Christ in such a real way. And this man was privileged to be among the first to receive this gift of salvation won by Jesus on the Cross.

Jesus offers us the same assurance. He offers salvation to us beginning today. And He offers it to us in the midst of our own suffering and sin. Can you hear Him offer you this gift of mercy? Can you hear Him invite you to share His gift of everlasting life? Let Him speak this invitation to you and let the eternal life of paradise begin to take hold more deeply today in your soul.

"Woman, behold your son."

What a gift! Here, dying on the Cross, Jesus entrusted His own mother to John. And in so doing, He entrusted her to each one of us. Our unity with Jesus makes us a member of His family and, thus, sons and daughters of His own mother. Our Blessed Mother accepts this responsibility with great joy. She embraces us and holds us close.

Do you accept Jesus' mother as your own spiritual mother? Have you fully consecrated yourself to her? Doing so will place you under her mantle of protection and love.

"My God, my God, why have you forsaken me?"

Jesus was not abandoned but He allowed Himself to feel and experience this complete loss of the Father in His human nature. He felt the deep experience of despair. He allowed Himself to know and experience the effects of sin. Therefore, He knows what we go through when we despair. He knows what it feels like. And He is there with us in those temptations enabling us to press on through any despair toward total faith and trust in the Father.

"I thirst."

What a meaningful statement. He thirsted physically at that moment for water to quench His dehydration. But more than that, He thirsted spiritually for the salvation of all of our souls. Jesus' spirit still longs for this gift of salvation. He longs to call us His children. He thirsts for our love.

Ponder Jesus saying these words to you. "I thirst for you!" He says. It is a deep and burning thirst for your love. You satiate Jesus' thirst by returning that love. Satiate His thirst this Good Friday by giving Him your love.

"Father, into your hands I commend my spirit."

These are the words we need to pray more than any. These are the words of complete surrender to God. Prayer is ultimately about one thing. It's about surrender. It's about trust. Say these words over and over today and let this perfect surrender of Jesus also be your surrender.

Surrender means God is in control. It means that we let go of our own will and choose only God's. And it means that God pledges to accept our surrender and guide us into the perfect plan He has in mind for us.

"It is finished."

It's significant that He said "It is finished" as His last words. What does this mean? What is finished?

This spiritual statement from Jesus is one that affirms that His mission of the redemption of the whole world is accomplished. "It" refers to His perfect sacrifice of love offered for all of us. His death, which we commemorate today, is the perfect sacrifice which takes away the sins of all. What a gift! And what a sacrifice Jesus endured for us!

We are used to seeing this sacrifice on the Cross. We ponder this sacrifice every time we look at the crucifix. But it is important to note that our over-familiarity with the Cross can tempt us to lose sight of the sacrifice. It's easy for us to miss what Jesus actually did for us. He accomplished the act that saves us and He is now offering it to us. Let this completed act of Divine Mercy penetrate your soul. He desires to say that His sacrifice has "finished" its work in your soul.

So today, on this Good Friday, it would be good if we spent the day pondering the reality of Jesus' sacrifice. Try to understand what it was like for God Himself to suffer and die. Contemplate what it was like for God Himself, the Creator of all things, to be put to death by those whom He created, to suffer at the hands of those whom He loved with a perfect love.

Understanding Jesus' sacrificial love will enable us to love as He did. It will enable us to love those who have hurt us and those who persecute us. His love is total. It is generous beyond description.

My crucified Lord, I know You thirst for my soul. You finished what You started by dying on the Cross for my salvation and the salvation of the world. Help me to understand Your love and to accept it into my life. Help me to forgive. Help me to invite You into my own darkness and sin. Help me to abandon all to You. I thank You, dear suffering Lord, for the gift of Your Precious Blood, poured out for the salvation of the world. Jesus, I trust in You.

A Prayer From the Cross

Good Friday of the Lord's Passion (Reflection Two)

> Father, into your hands I commend my spirit. Luke 23:46

One of the most profound and transforming prayers we could ever pray is given to us today as the response to our Psalm: "Father, into your hands I commend my spirit." These words were, of course, spoken by our Lord as He hung upon the Cross and prepared to breathe His last. But they are also words that echoed throughout the earthly life of Jesus, and they continue to echo from the divine heart of our Lord in Heaven for all eternity. "Father, into your hands I commend my spirit."

This prayer is a prayer of surrender to the perfect will of the Father in Heaven, which was the one and only mission of Jesus as He lived upon earth. His only goal was to fulfill the Father's will, and this was done by His continual surrender of His life to the Father. But Jesus' surrender to the Father in Heaven did not end as He died upon the Cross. His surrender to the Father is an eternal reality. He continually gives Himself to the Father with perfect love. This is Heaven. Heaven is an eternal unity of the Most Holy Trinity. It's an eternal giving of the Father to the Son and the Son to the Father. This perfect giving and receiving of love between the Father and the Son spirates the Holy Spirit Who proceeds from them both.

Imagine the response that the Father gave to the Son as He prayed this prayer from the Cross. Though the Father's response is not recorded in Scripture, we can be certain that the Father's response was one of complete receptivity and reciprocity. The Father received His eternal Son through that prayer and accepted the ultimate sacrifice of His earthly life for the salvation of the world. And the Father then responded in a reciprocal way by bestowing upon the Son in His human nature the full gift of His very self. Though the Father and the Son were always perfectly united as one, this prayer from the Cross became an earthly manifestation of this holy union.

Though this eternal reality of the Love of the Father, Son and Holy Spirit is a deep mystery of our faith, it is also a mystery that we must seek to penetrate and participate in. Heaven will be our eternal participation in this perfect love. Jesus' prayer on the Cross is the perfect prayer for us to pray throughout our lives so as to begin to enter into that eternal reality, here and now, and to prepare ourselves to share in this eternal union forever.

On this Good Friday, as you gaze upon the crucifixion of Jesus and reflect upon His brutal agony and His earthly death, try to look beyond His human suffering to His perfect surrender. Try to see that His physical death was nothing other than an act of perfect love for the Father and an act into which we are invited to participate. Prayerfully ponder this beautiful prayer of Jesus today: "Father, into your hands I commend my spirit." Say it over and over. Pray it slowly and meditatively. Savor each and every word. Make it your own prayer. Let it come forth from the depths of your spirit. Let it be your act of love of God so that the Holy Spirit will become manifest in your life. Use this prayer to show your love for the Father, making Him more fully your Father. Use this prayer as a way of uniting yourself with the eternal Son. Say it with Him, in Him and through Him. Strive to become one with our Lord as He manifests His oneness with the Father and the Holy Spirit. Share in Their divine life. If you do so from the depths of your being, you can be sure that our Father in Heaven will receive you just as He did His Son and They, together with the Holy Spirit, will bestow upon you the gift of their Triune life.

Father in Heaven, into Your hands I commend my spirit. As I gaze upon the crucifix and see Your eternal Son looking to You in Heaven, I unite myself with His eternal surrender to You. My Lord, Jesus, draw me into Your surrender and help me to make Your perfect prayer my own. I love You, Most Holy Trinity, and pray that I may share in the eternal reality of Your love. Jesus, I trust in You.

The Silence of the Tomb

Holy Saturday

Today, there is a great silence. The Savior has died. He rests in the tomb. Many hearts were filled with uncontrollable grief and confusion. Was He really gone? Had all their hopes been shattered? These and many other thoughts of despair filled the minds and hearts of so many who loved and followed Jesus.

It is on this day that we honor the fact that Jesus was still preaching. He descended to the land of the dead, to all the holy souls who had gone before Him, so as to bring them His gift of salvation. He brought His gift of mercy and redemption to Moses, Abraham, the prophets and so many others. This was a day of great joy for them. But a day of great sorrow and confusion for those who watched their Messiah die on the Cross.

It's helpful to ponder this apparent contradiction. Jesus was accomplishing His act of redemption, the greatest act of love ever known, and so many were in complete confusion and despair. It shows that God's ways are so far above our own ways. What appeared to be a great loss actually turned into the most glorious triumph ever known.

So it is with our lives. Holy Saturday should be a reminder to us that even those things which seem to be the worst of tragedies are not always what they seem. God the Son was obviously doing great things as He laid in the tomb. He was accomplishing His mission of redemption. He was changing lives and pouring forth grace and mercy.

The message of Holy Saturday is clear. It's a message of hope. Not hope in a worldly sense, rather, it's the message of divine hope. Hope and trust in God's perfect plan. Hope in the fact that God always has a greater purpose. Hope in the fact that God uses suffering and, in this case, death as a powerful instrument of salvation.

Spend time in silence today. Try to enter into the reality of Holy Saturday. Let divine hope grow within you knowing that Easter is soon to come.

Lord or all hope, I thank You for the gift of Your suffering and death. Thank You for this day of silence as we await Your Resurrection. May I also await Your triumph in my life. When I struggle with despair, dear Lord, help me to be reminded of this day. The day when all appeared as loss. Help me to see my struggles through the lens of Holy Saturday, remembering that You are faithful in all things and that the Resurrection is always assured to those who put their trust in You. Jesus, I do trust in You.

Octave of Easter

The Lord has Risen! Alleluia!

Easter Sunday (Year A)

> And behold, there was a great earthquake; for an angel of the Lord descended from heaven, approached, rolled back the stone, and sat upon it. His appearance was like lightning and his clothing was white as snow. The guards were shaken with fear of him and became like dead men. Then the angel said to the women in reply, "Do not be afraid! I know that you are seeking Jesus the crucified. He is not here, for he has been raised just as he said." Matthew 28:2–6b

What an experience that must have been! Mary Magdalene and the other Mary went to the tomb early in the morning to pay tribute to our Lord's sacred body. They brought the oils and perfumes that they planned on placing on his beaten and bruised body. They came to offer Him their last act of love. But as the women arrived, the earth quaked and the angel of God appeared to them.

As they left, Scripture says they then left the tomb quickly, "fearful yet overjoyed." All they could think about was telling the other disciples of their encounter when another incredible joy befell them. Jesus Himself met them on the way. In their amazement, the women fell at His feet and did Him homage. Not the homage they planned on doing to a dead body, but the homage due to a risen Savior. They worshipped Him. Jesus then spoke: "Do not be afraid. Go tell my brothers to go to Galilee, and there they will see me" (Mt. 28:10).

It was true. All they had hoped for came true. They saw Jesus arrested. They saw Him beaten. They saw Him falsely accused. They saw Him sentenced to death. And they saw

Him die. Now for the miracle of miracles, they saw their Savior alive. Every hope that they had came true. Everything came to fruition in that moment. All that was lost was restored a hundredfold.

The Resurrection of Christ is not simply an event that took place long ago. It's an event that continues to take place when we patiently walk with our Lord through the trials, crosses and sufferings of life, with hope and trust in His power to do all good things. Evil always loses in the end when we remain steadfast in our hope in Him.

As we celebrate the reality of the Resurrection of Christ, ponder the promise He has spoken to you. If you have surrendered all to Him and died to the world of sin, keep your eyes now on the Resurrection. Have hope in Him and in His power to breathe new life into your heaviest cross.

Sometimes we have hope in our own ideas of the Resurrection. We ask for some hope to come true because we think it is what we need. But the Resurrection of Christ should teach us that His plan for new life for each one of us is far superior than what we could ever imagine. Do you believe that? Do you maintain your hope in Christ even when all seems lost?

Reflect, today, upon the unfathomable plan that God has for your life. Know that if you remain faithful until the end, our Lord will bring forth greater joys in your life than you could ever think possible. It may not happen according to your schedule or your wishes, but it will happen in accord with His perfect divine will. Do not doubt. Do not be afraid. Have hope and trust, and anticipate the moments when the power of the Resurrection brings forth the greatest joys you could ever imagine.

My Resurrected Lord, I trust You with all my mind, heart, soul and strength. I believe that You are faithful to perfection and that Your fidelity will never fail. Give me hope when I need it the most and help me to keep my eyes on the glory that awaits. You have conquered all evil. May I always trust in You!

A New Day has Dawned

Easter Sunday (Year B)

> This is the day the Lord has made; let us rejoice and be glad. (see Psalm 118)

Our Easter celebration has begun! Happy Easter!

In many parts of the world, Easter comes in spring. It's the time of year when nature itself brings forth the beginnings of new life. The tulips begin to rise from the cold and dormant earth, the leaves begin to bud on the trees, transforming the forest into a sea of green, and the Sun begins to shine with a new radiance, sending warmth at its rising each morning. Creation itself reflects the glory and splendor of the Resurrection of Christ in many ways.

The death of winter reflects the death of Christ and the silence of the tomb experienced on Holy Saturday. Everything goes dormant. Vegetation appears to die, and even the animals and insects retreat into various forms of hibernation and immobility. However, at the appointed time, as the warmth of the Sun rises anew, nature itself is called forth from the death of winter into the new life of spring.

The cold winter would be deeply depressing if it were to remain forever. Just imagine if scientists were to tell us that the forthcoming winter was a unique one in that it would now remain forever. Never again would we see the warmth of spring or summer. Never again would we see the insects, plants and leaves on the trees. What a hopeless situation that would be!

Lent and Easter Reflections

But God speaks to us in many and varied ways, and one such way is through the cycle of nature. New life is certain! The warmth will return after the winter freeze, nature will rise and the earth will sing again.

If the Father in Heaven is so diligent about caring for the natural creation, how much more does He care for the recreation of humanity? How much more would He have cared for the Resurrection of His own divine Son? How much more does He care for our entrance into the new life won for each of us by the Resurrection of Jesus Christ from the dead?!

Allow the beauty of creation to be a sign to you of a reality that is infinitely greater. Allow yourself to be drawn into the newness of life that is bestowed upon you by your sharing in the Resurrection of Christ. To rise with Him means you are to become a new creation.

Reflect, today, upon the above line from the Responsorial Psalm for today's Mass. "This is the day the Lord has made; let us rejoice and be glad." The "day" we rejoice in is the new life God wants to bestow upon your soul here and now. It's a new day, a glorious one, a transformed one, a resurrected one. New life must begin now and must become continually new and glorious as we journey deeper and deeper into the glory of the Resurrection. Ponder this "new day" and allow our Lord to bestow it upon you through the power of His glorious Resurrection from the dead.

My resurrected Lord, my hope is in You! Alleluia, You are alive and You have conquered all sin, all death, all evil. You bring forth new life to all who turn to You in their need. My Jesus, I do turn to You and abandon myself to You in Your death so that I may rise with You in Your Resurrection to new life. Breathe into me this gift of new life and allow me to begin anew. Jesus, I trust in You.

Happy Easter!

Easter Sunday (Year C)

Alleluia! He is Risen!

Saying those words is like drinking a tall glass of cold water after being out in the desert all day. Lent is over and it is now time to celebrate the great joy of Easter!

At the Easter Vigil, the Exsultet is sung as Mass begins in darkness, illumined only by candles throughout the church. The Exsultet is a beautiful hymn of rejoicing in Christ's triumph over sin and death. One part states:

> O truly necessary sin of Adam, destroyed completely by the Death of Christ! O happy fault that earned for us so great, so glorious a Redeemer!

This line stands out because it calls the sin of Adam "necessary" and refers to it as "O happy fault." At first, this may seem strange. Why is it that we refer to the sin of Adam, Original Sin, as "necessary" and "happy." The answer is Easter. It's because God, in His perfect wisdom and love, took sin and the consequence of sin (death) and used them as the means of the salvation of the world. That's what Easter is all about!

This may be hard to comprehend so it's worth thinking about more deeply. Without Adam's sin, there would be no Jesus. God would not have had to become one of us. So even though the original sin of Adam, as well as all future sin, is evil and wrong, God in His perfect power and love chose to use it as the very means of the salvation of the world. How? By allowing the sins of the world to persecute Him and crucify Him, and then, by turning that suffering and death into the very means of salvation. Jesus destroyed sin by destroying the consequences of sin which is death. Death loses in the Resurrection! Jesus' Resurrection takes away the effects of all sin for those who cling to Him.

Easter is a time when we must do just that. We must "cling" to our resurrected Lord! We must cling to Jesus who is alive and well. We must cling to His Resurrection and strive to share in it. How do we cling to our Resurrected Lord? There are many ways. Here is one.

Take joy in everything. Start with whatever it is that burdens you the most. Whatever it is that makes you angry, sad or depressed. Whatever that is, it can potentially become one of your greatest sources of grace and joy. Seriously, it can. If the brutal Crucifixion of Jesus, the Son of God, can turn out to be the greatest event in all of human history, then your personal suffering, your burden, or even your sin can very much become a source of great joy as long as you let God transform it into part of His Resurrection!

This is the meaning of Easter! Easter means that nothing can keep us from the joy that God wants to give us. Nothing can steal that joy away. Sure, at times we will struggle just as Jesus did in the Agony of the Garden and the *Via Dolorosa* (the Way of the Cross), but those sufferings will not win. The Resurrection won with Christ and it will win with us when we cling to Him. Jesus persevered and, in the end, rose victorious. This is Easter!

Know that God wants you to experience the joy of Easter in your life. Let Him fill you with hope and with the joy that only the Resurrection can bring. God wants Easter to begin now in our lives! Happy Easter!

My transforming Lord, help me to cling to You in Your Resurrection. Help me to let you transform every cross and burden in my life into joy. Lord, may Your joy fill my life and be my strength in all things. Jesus, I trust in You.

Overjoyed at the Resurrection!
Monday in the Octave of Easter

> Mary Magdalene and the other Mary went away quickly from the tomb, fearful yet overjoyed, and ran to announce the news to his disciples. And behold, Jesus met them on their way and greeted them. Matthew 28:8–9

They went away "fearful" but also "overjoyed." What a fascinating combination! These two experiences do not at first seem like they go hand in hand. How is one fearful while also filled with joy? Wouldn't fear undermine joy? And wouldn't joy seem to cast out fear? This all depends upon what sort of "fear" these holy women were experiencing.

It seems that the fear these women were experiencing was one of the Seven Gifts of the Holy Spirit, the gift of holy fear. This is not a fear in the normal sense of being afraid. Rather, it's a fear that is better defined as a deep reverence, wonder and awe. It's a gift that enabled these women to recognize the profundity of what they were presently experiencing. They were in awe, holy shock, amazement and filled with joy all at the same time. They would have suddenly experienced the amazing realization and hope that Jesus had beaten death itself. They were most likely confused but also filled with a faith that left them with a conviction that something extraordinary had just taken place.

This is the experience we must have today. Today is the second day in the Octave of Easter. That means today is Easter Day once again. We celebrate Easter Day for eight straight days culminating with Divine Mercy Sunday. So these next eight days are days when we should spend extra time trying to penetrate and experience the same experience these holy women had as they first discovered that Jesus was no longer in the tomb. We must let ourselves engage the mystery of the Resurrection. We must see it for what it is. We must strive to comprehend this gift and the amazing fact that in His Resurrection, Jesus destroys the effects of sin. He destroys death itself. Truly amazing!

Do you understand the Resurrection of Christ? Not well enough. It's only the humble truth for each of us to admit that we need to understand the Resurrection more. We must let not only the truth of the Resurrection sink in, we must also allow the effects of the Resurrection to change us. We must allow the Resurrection of Christ to enter into our souls and invite us to share in this new life today.

As these holy women left the tomb, the Scripture tells us that they met the Resurrected Christ on their way. And it tells us that when they saw Jesus they, "approached, embraced his feet, and did him homage." This is no small act of adoration and love. This act of worship and adoration of Jesus shows that they not only believed, but also acted by worshiping Him. We must do the same.

Reflect, today, upon the awesome event of the Resurrection and spend time this week in this humble adoration. Try to literally bow down to the ground in homage before the Resurrected Christ. Try to do this literally. Perhaps in the silence of your room, or in a church, or any place that you can comfortably express this literal and physical act of worship and adoration. As you do this, let yourself come face to face with the Risen Lord. And let Him begin to more deeply transform your life!

Lord, I do believe. I believe You rose victorious over sin and death. Allow me, especially during this Octave of Easter, to enter into the great mystery of Your Resurrection. Help me to understand and experience this overwhelming glory in my life. I adore You with a profound love, dear Lord. Help me to worship You with all my might. Jesus, I trust in You.

Holding On to Jesus
Tuesday in the Octave of Easter

> Jesus said to her, "Woman, why are you weeping? Whom are you looking for?" She thought it was the gardener and said to him, "Sir, if you carried him away, tell me where you laid him, and I will take him. Jesus said to her, "Mary!" She turned and said to him in Hebrew, "Rabbouni," which means Teacher. Jesus said to her, "Stop holding on to me, for I have not yet ascended to the Father." John 20:15–17

Mary Magdalene had been outside Jesus' tomb weeping because she didn't know what had happened to His sacred body. Jesus appears to her suddenly in her grief and she is overwhelmed, crying out "Rabbouni!" Jesus tells her to stop holding on to Him. Why would Jesus say this? What did He mean?

As we can imagine, this was a very emotional moment for Mary. She had been there watching the entire Crucifixion. She knew Jesus well and loved Him dearly. She watched Him die and now, all of a sudden, Jesus was alive and in her presence. Her emotions must have been overwhelming.

Jesus was not being critical of Mary when He told her not to hold on to Him. He was actually giving her beautiful advice and direction in her spiritual journey and in her relationship with Him. He was telling her that His relationship was now going to change, and deepen. He told her not to hold on to Him because He had "not yet ascended to the Father." At that moment, Mary's relationship with Jesus was primarily on a human level. She had spent much time with Him, been in His physical presence, and loved Him with her human heart. But Jesus wanted more. He wanted her, and all of us, to now love Him in a divine way. He was soon to ascend to the Father, and from His heavenly throne He could descend to begin a new relationship with Mary, and with all of us, that was far more than one on a human level. From His throne in Heaven He could now enter Mary's soul. He could enter into a new and much deeper communion with her and with all of us. He could live in us and we in Him. He could become one with us.

By letting go of the more human and emotional aspects of her relationship with Jesus, Mary could soon cling to Him in a way that she couldn't do through her human interaction with Him. This is the divine marriage, the divine communion to which we are all called.

Reflect, today, upon your own clinging to Jesus. He is now fully resurrected and ascended and we can experience the full fruits of the Resurrection as a result. We, with Mary, can now hold on to Him in our souls because He is primarily the one holding on to us.

My exalted Lord, may I cling to You as You cling to me. May my heart, mind and soul be Yours. Come live in me so that I may live in You. I give my life to You, dear Lord, help me to offer You all that I am. Jesus, I trust in You.

Recognizing Jesus in Your Daily Life

Wednesday in the Octave of Easter

> That very day, the first day of the week, two of Jesus' disciples were going to a village seven miles from Jerusalem called Emmaus, and they were conversing about all the things that had occurred. And it happened that while they were conversing and debating, Jesus himself drew near and walked with them, but their eyes were prevented from recognizing him. Luke 24:13–16

This appearance of Jesus to two of His disciples is intriguing and fascinating. They were quite distraught and didn't seem to know what to think about Jesus' death. They had hoped He was the Messiah but then He was killed. And then there were some who claimed His tomb was empty. What should they make of all this?

As the story goes on, Jesus "interpreted to them what referred to him in all the Scriptures." With that, these disciples realized that this man with whom they were speaking had incredible wisdom and understanding, so they invited Him to stay with them. Jesus stayed and sat down with them in their home. While there, Scripture says that "he took bread, said the blessing, broke it, and gave it to them. With that their eyes were opened and they recognized him, but he vanished from their sight."

Again, this is intriguing and fascinating. Why did Jesus appear to them, conceal who He was, sit down and break bread with them, allow them to suddenly recognize Him and then vanish into thin air? Well, He did it for a reason and we should be very attentive to this.

Jesus wanted those disciples, as well as all of us, to know that He who rose from the dead was very much alive and that we would recognize Him in the breaking of the bread. We would recognize Him in the Most Holy Eucharist!

This appearance of Jesus to these disciples was, in fact, an appearance to teach all of us the simple truth of His presence in the Eucharist. It was at that moment, as they "took bread, said the blessing, broke it," that Jesus was suddenly made manifest to their minds and souls. Jesus is alive in the Eucharist! But it also tells us that He is veiled in the Eucharist. This combination of being veiled and truly present gives us wonderful guidance in our faith.

Jesus is here, right now, in our presence, but we most likely do not see Him. But He is truly here! These disciples were in the presence of Jesus and they did not realize it. The same is true for us. We are constantly in His presence and we do not realize it. This is especially true when we are at Mass but it is also true in countless other ways throughout our day. We must commit ourselves to seeing Him, to recognizing Him and to adoring Him. We must discover the resurrected presence of Jesus all around us.

Too often we think that our Lord is present only in extraordinary ways. But that is not true! He is constantly present to us in very ordinary ways. He is here with us right now, loving us, speaking to us, and calling us to love Him. Do you see Him? Do you recognize His presence?

Reflect, today, upon the experience of these disciples. If you were them, you'd be blessed to be in the presence of the Savior of the world. What an honor! The truth is that God is with you now and always. He is constantly with you and is constantly speaking with you. Look for Him and listen to His voice. You may be surprised at how near He really is.

My ever-present Lord, thank You for loving me so much that You are always with me. Help me to see You and to recognize Your gentle and still voice. Give me the eyes of faith to see You present in the Most Holy Eucharist, and help me to discern Your presence in every ordinary event of my day. I love You, dear Lord. Jesus, I trust in You.

Incredulous for Joy!

Thursday in the Octave of Easter

> While they were still incredulous for joy and were amazed, he asked them, "Have you anything here to eat?" They gave him a piece of baked fish; he took it and ate it in front of them. Luke 24:41–43

"Incredulous for joy!" What a great description of the disciples' reaction to Jesus! To be "incredulous" means that

Octave of Easter

the disciples were not sure what to believe. They were hesitant to believe in what they were seeing. There was Jesus, whom they saw crucified, standing before them with the wounds in His hands and feet. He was talking to them and asked for something to eat. They were in a bit of shock, disbelief and uncertainty.

But the description says that they were incredulous "for joy!" It's as if they were waiting to explode with joy, they wanted to experience joy in what they were seeing, but something was holding them back. It all seemed to be too good. Was it true? Could it be that Jesus really conquered death and was once again back with them?

This reaction of the disciples reveals an experience that we all have at times when invited by God to enter into His glory and grace. So often, when God invites us closer to Himself, when He invites us to experience the joy of His Resurrection, we react with hesitancy. We can find it hard to actually let ourselves experience the reality of the Resurrection in our lives.

This can happen for many reasons. Discouragement is one cause for our hesitancy to fully embrace the Resurrection. The disciples were deeply discouraged at the death of Jesus. And now that He had risen, and was standing there before them, they were hesitant to let go of that discouragement they let take hold.

So also, we can easily let the weight of the world, our sin, or the sins of others get to us. We can get angry or upset and find ourselves brewing over the apparent problems we face. Taking joy in the Resurrection means we turn our eyes away from those things and look intently at the realities God wants us to focus on. It does no good to become discouraged with the many problems that come our way. Instead, our Lord is regularly calling us to look beyond them to something greater. He is calling us to look to His victory!

Looking at His victory is freeing and produces an incredible faith in our lives. And that faith in the Risen Lord will have the effect of a wonderful joy that God wants us to have.

Reflect, today, upon your own reaction to the reality of the Resurrection of our Lord. Spend some time today gazing upon the Risen Lord. Look at His victory. Look at His glory. Look at Him who calls you to a deep faith. With your eyes fixed on Him, all else that tempts you to discouragement simply fades away.

My resurrected Lord, I do want to gaze upon You. I want to see Your splendor and glory. I want to see You risen from the dead and take great joy and delight in this reality. Help me, dear Lord, to experience the incredible joy that comes from knowing You, our Resurrected Lord. Jesus, I trust in You.

Fishing for Souls with Jesus

Friday in the Octave of Easter

> "Cast the net over the right side of the boat and you will find something." So they cast it, and were not able to pull it in because of the number of fish. John 21:6

Every fisherman would love to have the experience that Jesus offered the Apostles in the passage above. The Apostles were fishing all night and caught nothing. Then, in the morning, Jesus appeared on the shore but they did not realize it was Him. He then gave them a simple command to cast their net off the right side of the boat. And they caught so many fish they could not pull them in. What an exciting catch!

This catch of fish was much more than just a favor from Jesus to help them with their work. It was highly symbolic. The central symbolism is that Jesus was giving the Apostles a new calling. They would no longer be fishing just for fish, rather, they were now to fish for souls. And the important part is that if they attempted to do this by their own efforts, they would come up empty handed. If, however, they did it at the Lord's command, in His way, within His timing, then their efforts would provide an abundance of good fruit. More than they could ever imagine!

This miracle of Jesus begins to reveal to the Apostles (and to us) the command that comes to evangelize the world. This revelation comes after His Resurrection as Jesus gives His final instructions to the Apostles to carry out His mission of salvation. We should see in this miracle our own call to spread the Good News. And we must see in this miracle the command to spread the Good News only at the command of Jesus, in His way and within His timing.

Sometimes Christians tend to come up with many "good" ideas to spread the Gospel. But the key is to humble ourselves before God and realize that we are incapable of spreading the Good News of the Gospel unless the Lord is leading the way and giving the direction. This tells us we should wait on Him and let Him speak. We must listen to His voice and respond only when He leads. Evangelization is a response to Jesus rather than something we do by our own effort. This is the central message of this miraculous event.

As we continue our Easter Day celebration, it is a good time for each of us to reflect upon our own responsibility to evangelize. We all have a calling to share in this work of Jesus. It will take on different forms for each of us according to our vocation and mission. But the real question is this: "Am I responding to the call from Jesus to evangelize in the way He is directing me?" This is an important question. We should know that the particular mission Jesus gives us is not entrusted to anyone else. And He does want to use us.

Reflect, today, upon this command our Lord gave to the Apostles and hear Him speak this same command to you, calling you to "fish for souls" in accord with His holy will. Let the Lord speak to you this week and let yourself be open to His direction. God wants to use you, so make sure you let Him!

My commanding Lord, I do want to be used by You. I do want to evangelize in accord with Your will. Help me to confidently answer the call, and help me to sincerely listen to the direction You give. Use me, dear Lord, to save many souls for Your Kingdom. Jesus, I trust in You.

Softening Your Heart

Saturday in the Octave of Easter

> But later, as the Eleven were at table, he appeared to them and rebuked them for their unbelief and hardness of heart because they had not believed those who saw him after he had been raised. Mark 16:14

Why did the Apostles fail to believe Jesus had risen from the dead? They had seen so many amazing miracles first hand from Jesus. They lived with Him day in and day out for three years. They heard Him preach and teach with perfect authority and grace. And now, after He rose from the dead, their hearts were hardened and they did not immediately believe. Jesus had to appear to them and offer this proof to their own eyes.

This struggle that the Apostles went through is one that is all too common. It's the struggle of a hardness of heart. They wanted to believe, but they couldn't let themselves freely embrace the Resurrection with true faith until they had some proof. Little did they know that all the proof they needed was already within them.

So often we are invited by Jesus to have faith and believe in Him and to accept many things as a matter of faith. The gift of faith is like a small flame within our hearts that we carelessly expose to the winds. This carelessness allows the flame of faith to be extinguished before it can grow.

The goal of our Christian walk is to let that flame of faith become the blazing fire that God wants. And it's possible! It's entirely possible to let that flame become so all-consuming that nothing can put it out. Are you willing to do what you need to so as to let that flame glow brightly? And how do we do this?

The path to this blazing fire of faith within has to do with the way we handle that spark which is already there. We have to care for and nurture that small flame. We have to treat the beginnings of our faith with great care. We must guard it and feed it so that it grows. This is done, in part, by avoiding carelessness in our life of prayer.

Prayer is the key to letting God grow within. He is there, speaking to us and calling us to believe. Every time we doubt, or harden our heart, we expose that tiny flame to the elements. But every time we intensely focus upon that flame, we enable it to grow and take hold. Praying, listening, seeking, loving and believing are the ways to the faith God wants to bestow upon us. And if the Apostles would have just let that gift of faith, planted deep within, grow by a softening of their hearts, they would have quickly and easily believed that Jesus was alive without having a need to see Him with their own eyes.

Reflect, today, upon the fact that we do not see the Resurrected Christ in a physical way, but we do have the same ability as the Apostles to know and love Him. What are you doing every day to let this love and knowledge of Christ grow? What are you doing in your own faith life to let this flame become a blazing and all-consuming fire?

Recommit yourself this day to prayer, and watch your faith in Christ grow brightly!

Lord, I love You and I believe in You. Help me to fan the flame of faith planted in my heart into a blazing and all-consuming fire. Help me to know and love You so that this knowledge and love transform me. Purify my soul by this fire and free me from any hardness of heart. Jesus, I trust in You.

The Divine Mercy

Divine Mercy Sunday (Year A)

> On that day all the divine floodgates through which graces flow are opened. Let no soul fear to draw near to Me, even though its sins be as scarlet. My mercy is so great that no mind, be it of man or of angel, will be able to fathom it throughout all eternity. Everything that exists has come forth from the very depths of My most tender mercy. Every soul in its relation to Me will contemplate My love and mercy throughout eternity. The Feast of Mercy emerged from My very depths of tenderness. It is My desire that it be solemnly celebrated on the first Sunday after Easter. Mankind will not have peace until it turns to the Fount of My Mercy. (*Diary of Divine Mercy* #699)

This message, spoken by Jesus to Saint Faustina in 1931, has now come true. What was spoken in the solitude of a cloistered convent in Płock Poland, now is celebrated by the Universal Church throughout the whole world!

Saint Maria Faustina Kowalska of the Blessed Sacrament was known to very few people during her lifetime. But through her, God has spoken the message of His abundant mercy to the entire Church and world. What is this message? Though its content is endless and unfathomable, here are five key ways that Jesus desires this new devotion to be lived:

The first way is through *meditation on the sacred image of The Divine Mercy*. Saint Faustina was asked by Jesus to have an image of His merciful love painted for all to see. It's an image of Jesus with two rays shining forth from His Heart. The first ray is blue, indicating the font of Mercy coming forth through Baptism; and the second ray is red, indicating the font of Mercy poured forth through the Blood of the Holy Eucharist.

The second way is *through the celebration of Divine Mercy Sunday*. Jesus told Saint Faustina that He desired an annual solemn Feast of Mercy. This Solemnity of Divine Mercy was established as a universal celebration on the Eighth day of the Octave of Easter. On that day the floodgates of Mercy are opened and many souls are made holy.

The third way is *through the Chaplet of Divine Mercy*. The chaplet is a treasured gift. It's a gift that we should seek to pray each and every day.

The fourth way is *by honoring the hour of Jesus' death every day*. It was at 3 o'clock that Jesus took His last breath and died upon the Cross. It was Friday. For this reason, Friday should always be seen as a special day to honor His Passion and ultimate Sacrifice. But since it took place at 3 o'clock, it is also important to honor that hour each and every day. This is the ideal time to pray the Chaplet of Divine Mercy. If the Chaplet is not possible, it's at least important to pause and give thanks to our Lord every day at that time.

The fifth way is *through the Apostolic Movement of The Divine Mercy*. This movement is a call from our Lord to actively engage in the work of spreading His Divine Mercy. This is done by spreading the message and by living Mercy toward others.

On this, the Eighth Day of the Octave of Easter, Divine Mercy Sunday, ponder the above desires of the heart of Jesus. Do you believe that the message of Divine Mercy is meant not only for you but also for the whole world? Do you seek to understand and incorporate this message and devotion into your life? Do you seek to become an instrument of mercy to others? Become a disciple of The Divine Mercy and seek to spread this Mercy in the ways given to you by God.

My merciful Lord, I trust in You and in Your abundant Mercy! Help me, this day, to deepen my devotion to Your merciful heart and to open my soul to the treasures that pour forth from this font of Heavenly riches. May I trust You, Love You and become an instrument of You and Your Mercy to the whole world. Jesus, I trust in You!

The Feast of Mercy

Divine Mercy Sunday (Year B)

Saint Faustina writes in her *Diary:*

> On one occasion, I heard these words: "My daughter, tell the whole world about My Inconceivable mercy. I desire that the Feast of Mercy be a refuge and shelter for all souls, and especially for poor sinners. On that day the very depths of My tender mercy are open. I pour out a whole ocean of graces upon those souls who approach the fount of My mercy. The soul that will go to Confession and receive Holy Communion shall obtain complete forgiveness of sins and punishment. On that day all the divine floodgates through which grace flow are opened (*Diary* #699).

It was Jesus Himself, through the mediation of this humble and holy religious sister, Sister Maria Faustina Kowalska of the Blessed Sacrament, Who instituted the Feast of Mercy that we celebrate today. In addition to the above quote from her *Diary of Divine Mercy*, Jesus spoke on numerous other occasions about His desire that this feast be instituted as a universal Feast of Mercy to be celebrated throughout the world on the eighth day of Easter every year.

From the time of her death in 1938, the private revelations from Jesus to Sister Faustina began to be read and shared. At first, the Feast of Mercy was celebrated by only a few who knew of these messages. As these private revelations began to circulate further, there were some within the Church who questioned their authenticity. Thus, on March 6, 1959, the writings of Sister Faustina were put on the "forbidden" list by the Holy Office, Rome. However, in 1965, with the permission of the same Holy Office, the Archbishop of Kraków, Poland, Archbishop Karol Wojtyła, began an informative process in which new light was shed upon Sister Faustina and her writings. This process concluded on April 15, 1978, with the Congregation for the Doctrine of the Faith, Rome, issuing a new decree permitting the spread of Sister Faustina's writings and the new devotion to The Divine Mercy. Then, by the providence of God, just six months later, the Archbishop of Kraków, Karol Wojtyła, was elected pope, taking the name Pope John Paul II. A little over two decades later, on April 30, 2000, Sister Faustina was canonized a saint in a ceremony presided over by Pope John Paul II. During her canonization, the Holy Father also instituted the Feast of Mercy for the universal Church to be celebrated on the eighth day of the Octave of Easter every year.

The providence of God is truly amazing. God started with this humble cloistered nun. He allowed His private revelations to be scrutinized by the Church and ultimately hand picked one of the greatest popes our Church has ever known to introduce these private revelations to the world. It's amazing to ponder the process by which these revelations went from the silent cloister of Sister Faustina to the universal Church. One thing this process truly tells us is that God must deeply desire that we immerse ourselves in the messages of Divine Mercy given through Saint Faustina. It was by God's providence that these messages slowly moved from the silence of the cloister in Kraków, Poland, to the universal Church beginning in the year 2000. Though it may be tempting to think that these messages are old and outdated, we should realize that God knew how long it would take for them to become instituted as a universal feast for all. Therefore, though these messages were first revealed before 1938, it was God's plan that they would especially be needed and read starting in the year 2000 and beyond. The message of Divine Mercy is especially for us today.

Reflect, today, upon this beautiful providence of God in bringing forth His message of mercy. Allow His providential methodology to not only inspire you but also to greatly encourage you to immerse yourself in the messages given to us from Jesus through Saint Faustina. Try to commit yourself to reading these messages so that, through them, God's providence will be able to come to fruition.

Most merciful God, You are The Divine Mercy, You are Mercy Itself. Help me to continually ponder this glorious gift of Your Mercy in my life. May the inspired writings of Saint Faustina especially be a gift to me so that their messages will bring forth Your mercy more fully in my life. Jesus, I trust in You.

The Mercy of God in Superabundance!
Divine Mercy Sunday (Year C)

What a grace-filled day this is! It is the eighth and final day of the Octave of Easter. On this eighth day of Easter we celebrate Divine Mercy Sunday. It is a day when the floodgates of mercy are opened wide and God lavishes us with more than we could ever hope for.

Divine Mercy Sunday has been celebrated for years as a private devotion. But in the year 2000, Pope Saint John Paul II, who himself was an extraordinary instrument of God's mercy, put this feast on the Church's official calendar as he raised Sister Faustina to sainthood.

Saint Faustina was a member of the Congregation of Sisters of Our Lady of Mercy in Krakow, Poland. She died in 1938. She came from a simple and poor family of farmers, had only three years of simple education and performed the humblest of tasks in her convent. But she also was a mystic who was privileged to have many private revelations from our Lord which she recorded in her diary of Divine Mercy.

She writes of her experience on February 22, 1931:

> In the evening, when I was in my cell, I became aware of the Lord Jesus clothed in a white garment. One hand was raised in blessing, the other was touching the garment at the breast. From the opening of the garment at the breast there came forth two large rays, one red and the other pale. In silence I gazed intently at the Lord; my soul was overwhelmed with fear, but also with great joy. After a while Jesus said to me, 'paint an image according to the pattern you see, with the inscription: Jesus, I trust in You.'

Later, Jesus explained to her in another vision:

> "The pale ray stands for the Water which makes souls righteous; the red ray stands for the Blood which is the life of souls. These two rays issued forth from the depths of My most tender Mercy at that time when My agonizing Heart was opened by a lance on the Cross....Fortunate is the one who will dwell in their shelter, for the just hand of God shall not lay hold of him."

Jesus spoke again to her of His desire that the Solemnity of Divine Mercy be established:

> "On that day (the 8th day of Easter each year) the very depths of My tender mercy are open. I pour out a whole ocean of graces upon those souls who approach the fount of My mercy. The soul that will go to Confession and receive Holy Communion shall obtain complete forgiveness of sins and punishment. On that day all the divine floodgates through which grace flow are opened. Let no soul fear to draw near to Me, even though its sins be as scarlet. My mercy is so great that no mind, be it of man or of angel, will be able to fathom it throughout all eternity."

As we celebrate Divine Mercy Sunday, intensely reflect upon the abundance of this gift that God wishes to pour forth upon us. There is no limit to how much we are loved by our God of perfect mercy. And today, on this the eighth day of Easter, we should especially be aware of the fact that the floodgates of Heaven are opened to us to an unimaginable degree. Turn your eyes toward our merciful Lord and be open to all that He wishes to bestow.

Lord of Mercy, help me today to begin to understand what mercy is all about. Help me to first be open to the mercy You wish to bestow upon me. As I receive Your own Divine Mercy, help me also to be an instrument of that mercy for all to see. Jesus, I trust in You.

+++

Prayer for Trust in The Divine Mercy of God

Most merciful Jesus,

I turn to You in my need.

You are worthy of my complete trust.

You are faithful in all things.

When my life is filled with confusion, give me clarity and faith.

When I am tempted to despair, fill my soul with hope.

Most merciful Jesus,

I trust You in all things.

I trust in Your perfect plan for my life.

I trust You when I cannot comprehend Your divine will.

I trust You when all feels lost.

Jesus, I trust You more than I trust myself.

Most merciful Jesus,

You are all-knowing.

Nothing is beyond Your sight.

You are all-loving.

Nothing in my life is beyond Your concern.

You are all-powerful.

Nothing is beyond Your grace.

Most merciful Jesus,

I trust in You,

I trust in You,

I trust in You.

May I trust You always and in all things.

May I daily surrender to Your Divine Mercy.

Most Blessed Virgin Mary, Mother of Mercy,

Pray for us as we turn to you in our need.

Amen.

Second Week of Easter

Born Again

Monday of the Second Week of Easter

> "Amen, amen, I say to you, unless one is born of water and Spirit he cannot enter the Kingdom of God." John 3:5

Are you born again? This is a common question among many evangelical Christians. But it's a question that we should ask ourselves also. So are you? And what does that exactly mean?

Hopefully each one of us answers that question with a wholehearted "Yes!" Scripture is clear that we must receive a new birth in Christ. The old self must die and the new self must be reborn. This is what it means to become a Christian. We take on a new life in Christ.

Being born again happens by water and the Holy Spirit. It happens in baptism. When we are baptized we enter into the waters and die with Christ. As we rise from the waters, we are reborn in Him. This means that baptism does something truly amazing in us. It means that, as a result of our baptism, we are adopted into the very life of the Most Holy Trinity. Baptism, for most of us, happened when we were infants. It's one of those things we do not think about very often. But we should.

Baptism is a sacrament that has an ongoing and eternal effect in our lives. It implants an indelible character upon our souls. This "character" is a constant source of grace in our lives. It is like a well of grace that never goes dry. From this well we are constantly nourished and renewed to live out the dignity we are called to live. We are given from this well the grace we need to live as sons and daughters of our Father in Heaven.

Reflect, today, upon your own Baptism. Easter is a time more than any when we are called to renew this Sacrament. Holy water is a good way to do just that. Perhaps the next time you are at church it would be good to consciously remind yourself of your baptism, and the dignity and grace you have been given through this sacrament, by making a sign of the cross on your forehead with holy water. Baptism has made you into a new creation. Seek to both understand and live that new life you have been given during this Easter season.

Heavenly Father, I renew today my baptism. I forever renounce sin and profess my faith in Christ Jesus Your Son. Give me the grace I need to live out the dignity to which I have been called. Jesus, I trust in You.

The Effects of the Holy Spirit

Tuesday of the Second Week of Easter

> Jesus said to Nicodemus: "'You must be born from above.' The wind blows where it wills, and you can hear the sound it makes, but you do not know where it comes from or where it goes; so it is with everyone who is born of the Spirit." John 3:7–8

Do you sense the presence of the Holy Spirit in your life? In this passage, Jesus offers an image of how the Holy Spirit works in us. He analogizes the Holy Spirit to the wind. We can hear the wind blowing but cannot see it. We do, however, perceive the effects of the wind. For example, when you see a tree swaying, you know that the wind is blowing.

So it is with the Holy Spirit in our lives. Though we may not be able to tangibly perceive where the Holy Spirit comes from, we will be able to see the effects of the Spirit. When we perceive a new strength within us, or an increase in virtues, or an ability to forgive, etc., we are aware of the fact that the Holy Spirit is present, leading us, transforming us and guiding us.

Additionally, we do not know where the wind goes once it passes. So it is with the Holy Spirit. If our lives are under the power and care of the Holy Spirit, we do not know where we will be led. The Holy Spirit leads us in the moment but does not typically reveal our whole future. We must be content to be led by the daily gentle presence of God, allowing ourselves to be moved here and there. This requires much trust and abandonment.

Reflect, today, upon the powerful presence of the Holy Spirit in your life. Look for the effects of the Holy Spirit to discern whether or not you are being truly led by God. Allow yourself to be led and moved by the Breath of God and anticipate great things in your life.

Come Holy Spirit, renew within me the grace of my Baptism and lead me each and every day in accord with Your divine will. I abandon myself to Your glorious care and trust in the promptings of Your presence in my life. Jesus, I trust in You.

What Do You Prefer?

Wednesday of the Second Week of Easter

> And this is the verdict, that the light came into the world, but people preferred darkness to light, because their works were evil. John 3:19

What a strange thing to be so true. God the Father sent the Son into the world to be Light for us all. He is the Light that dispels all darkness. But, according to the Gospel above, "people preferred darkness to light." They preferred their own sins to freedom from sin. Why is that?

As an example of this reality, all we have to do is watch the news or read the newspaper. It seems that 90% of what is reported in the news media is a sensationalistic presentation of darkness. We hear of one murder after another or one scandal after another. Why does the media focus upon this so much? Because it's what sells. And why does it sell? Because we too often are drawn to darkness more than we are to light.

Certainly that is not the case for everyone. So many are quite disinterested in the darkness of the world and the sensationalistic sins all around us. But the fact that the darkness of evil is so front and center all the time should offer us a certain warning about our fallen human nature. We tend to be drawn into mud and too often are all too happy there.

Easter is a time to examine what it is you are drawn to. Do you let yourself be drawn into the Light? Are you attracted by those things that brighten your day? Are you drawn to the many ways that God is present and active in the world all around you? Hopefully you are. But there is most likely some degree of pull toward disorder, sin and darkness. There can be an interior conflict that everyone experiences. It's good to be aware of this, to identify it as part of our fallen human tendency, and to seek to shed all interest in the chaos and evil all around us.

As a follower of Christ, we are called to keep our eyes on Him and on Him alone. We are called to penetrate the darkness with our faith and to let our whole being be attracted to and drawn toward Christ Jesus. Perfection means that even our passions and desires are ultimately drawn to Christ as the Light of our life.

Reflect, today, upon that which you are drawn toward the most. Commit yourself to the Light this Easter Season. Move your eyes from the temptation to become drawn in and fascinated by the evil around us, to the joyful vision of our Resurrected Lord alive and at work all around us. Let this Light guide your daily life.

Lord of Light, help me to live in Your light. Help me to keep my eyes firmly focused upon the glory of Your Resurrection. May the joy of that gaze keep me from the countless distractions of evil all around me. Jesus, I trust in You.

No Rationing of the Spirit
Thursday of the Second Week of Easter

He does not ration his gift of the Spirit. John 3:34

At wartime, when soldiers have a scarce amount of food, they have to ration it. They only eat small measured portions each day so that the food will last as long as possible. If they do not, they may run out and starve.

What if this were the case with God and His grace? What if the Holy Spirit were to say to us, "Now I'm only going to help you to a limited degree. Once you use up the grace I'm offering you, you're on your own." Ouch! That would be problematic.

Of course the good news is that God acts in the completely opposite way with us. He commits to a full outpouring of the Holy Spirit and offers all the grace we could ever need or want. The problem is that we often "ration" His grace anyway. We don't do this because we believe God is limited. Rather, we often do it because we are afraid to let God unleash His almighty power in our lives.

Reflect, today, upon what your life would look like if you let God do whatever He wanted with you. What would change? How would your daily life, your relationships, your words, your actions and your future be different? Intellectually speaking, we know it's right to fully embrace the will of God in all things. But when it actually comes to doing it, there is often much hesitancy. It may be fear of the unknown. Or it may be that we do not fully want to change. Whatever the case may be, God is offering you an unlimited amount of grace by the full outpouring of the Holy Spirit. It's up to you to decide if you will ration or not.

Lord of superabundance, I do want to let You do whatever You want in my life. I want to be fully immersed in Your grace. Help me to say "Yes" to You no matter what that leads to and help me to trust in this glorious "Yes" You are calling me to make. Jesus, I trust in You.

Being Tested

Friday of the Second Week of Easter

> When Jesus raised his eyes and saw that a large crowd was coming to him, he said to Philip, "Where can we buy enough food for them to eat?" He said this to test him, because he himself knew what he was going to do. John 6:5–6

God always knows what He is going to do. He always has a perfect plan for our lives. Always. In the passage above, we read a snippet from the miracle of the multiplication of the loaves and fish. Jesus knew He was going to multiply the few loaves and fish they had and feed over five thousand people. But before He did this, He wanted to test Philip, and so He did. Why does Jesus test Philip and why does He test us at times?

It's not that Jesus is curious about what Philip will say. And it's not that He is just playing games with Philip. Rather, He is seizing this opportunity to let Philip manifest His faith. So, in fact, this "testing" of Philip was a gift to him because it gave Philip the opportunity to pass the test.

The test was to let Philip act on faith rather than just on human logic alone. Sure, it's good to be logical. But very often the wisdom of God supersedes human logic. In other words, it brings logic to a whole new level. It brings it to a level where faith in God is brought into the equation.

So Philip, in that moment, was being called to offer a solution given the fact that the Son of God was there with them. And he fails the test. He points out that two hundred days' wages would not be enough to feed the crowd. But Andrew somewhat comes to the rescue. Andrew states that there is a boy who has a few loaves and some fish. Unfortunately he adds, "but what good are these for so many?"

This little spark of faith in Andrew, however, is enough faith for Jesus to have the crowds recline and to perform the miracle of the multiplication of the food. It seems that Andrew at least had a small insight into the fact that these few loaves and fish were important to mention. Jesus takes this from Andrew and takes care of the rest.

Reflect, today, upon the precious gift of even a little faith. So often we find ourselves in difficult situations where we don't know what to do. We should strive to have at least a little faith so that Jesus has something to work with. No, we may not have the full picture of what He wants to do, but we should at least have a small inkling of the direction God is leading. If we can at least manifest this little faith then we too will pass the test.

Lord, help me to have faith in Your perfect plan for my life. Help me to know that You are in control when life seems out of control. In those moments, may the faith I manifest be a gift to You so that You can use it for Your glory. Jesus, I trust in You.

Overcoming Daily Fear

Saturday of the Second Week of Easter

> When they had rowed about three or four miles, they saw Jesus walking on the sea and coming near the boat, and they began to be afraid. But he said to them, "It is I. Do not be afraid." John 6:19–20

This very familiar phrase was spoken once again: "Do not be afraid."

The setting is significant. It is dark and the Apostles are out to sea. If you've ever been out in the middle of the sea when it's dark out you'd know that this is a bit frightening. You cannot see the land and you feel as though you are surrounded by nothing. The Apostles would have been feeling a bit lost as if they were in the middle of nowhere.

But, in the midst of this experience, Jesus came walking to them and told them, "It is I. Do not be afraid." This would have been quite consoling to them.

We must see in this experience of the Apostles the daily experience so many have. Many can feel as if they are surrounded by nothing, alone and lost. Sure, this may not be an overwhelming feeling for some, but it is all too often an experience many do have to one degree or another.

This Gospel passage reveals to us that Jesus comes to us no matter where we are or whatever the situation is that we find ourselves in. He does not wait for us to come and find Him, rather, He enters into our lives right where we are.

This experience of being at sea in the dark comes in many forms. Perhaps your life is filled with activity, but you still feel alone. Perhaps your life is one where you do not have many around and feel the constant experience of isolation. Or perhaps you put on a good face and present yourself as one who has it all together, but inside you are deeply struggling. Whatever the case may be, Jesus wants to come to you and to console you.

Reflect, today, upon these words of Jesus. Listen to Him say to you, "It is I." As you hear Him say these words, turn to Him and acknowledge His presence. Let Him come into the dark sea that you may feel surrounds you. Hear Him say, "Do not be afraid." There are so many experiences in life that we can fear. So many times that fear can take hold of us. If we but let ourselves focus in on Jesus, the fear of our daily surroundings disappears. We discover, deep within, that Jesus is right there and that all is well because He cares and is in control. Let Him into the boat of your heart and let Him take over. He is coming to you and is waiting for a response.

Lord of all consolation, so often I fail to acknowledge Your divine presence in my life. So often I fail to see you coming to me. Help me to know that You are always there. Free me from the many fears of life, dear Lord, and give me courage to welcome You fully into my life. Jesus, I trust in You.

Third Week of Easter

The Gift of Understanding

Third Sunday of Easter (Years A)

> With that their eyes were opened and they recognized him, but he vanished from their sight. Then they said to each other, "Were not our hearts burning within us while he spoke to us on the way and opened the scriptures to us?" Luke 24:31–32 (Year A)

This passage above produced a unique blessing. Jesus opened the minds of the Apostles to the Scriptures in a new way. These were ordinary men who were given an extraordinary gift of understanding. It didn't come to them as a result of long study and hard work. Rather, it came to them as a result of their openness to Christ's powerful action in their lives. Jesus unlocked the mysteries of the Kingdom of Heaven to them. As a result, they suddenly understood truths that could never be learned on their own.

So it is with us. The mysteries of God are vast and wide. They are deep and transforming. But so often we fail to understand. We often even fail to want to understand.

Think about those things in your life now, or in your past, that have left you confused. You need a special gift of the Holy Spirit to make sense of them. And you need this gift to make sense of the many good things of God found in the Scriptures also. This is the Gift of Understanding. It's a spiritual gift that unlocks the many mysteries of life for us.

Without the Gift of Understanding, we are left on our own to try to make sense of life. This is especially true when we are faced with hardship and suffering. How is it, for example, that an all-powerful and all-loving God can allow the good and the innocent to suffer? How is it that God can seem absent at times from human tragedy?

The truth is that He is not absent. He is centrally involved in all things. What we need to receive is an understanding of the profound and mysterious ways of God. We need to understand the Scriptures, human suffering, human relationships, and divine action in our lives. But this will never happen unless we allow Jesus to open our minds.

Allowing Jesus to open our minds takes faith and surrender. It means we believe first and understand later. It means we trust Him even though we do not see. St. Augustine once said, "Faith is to believe what you do not see. The reward of faith is to see what you believe." Are you willing to believe without seeing? Are you willing to believe in the goodness and love of God even though life, or a particular situation in life, does not make sense?

Reflect, today, upon the Gift of Understanding. Believing in God means we believe in a person. We believe in Him even though we find ourselves confused about particular circumstances. But this gift of believing, the gift of faith, opens the door to a depth of understanding that we could never arrive at on our own.

God of all Truth, give me the Gift of Understanding. Help me to know You and to understand Your actions in my life. Help me to especially turn to You in the most troubling moments of life. Jesus, I trust in You.

Jesus' Parting Words

Third Sunday of Easter (Year B)

> Then he opened their minds to understand the Scriptures. And he said to them, "Thus it is written that the Christ would suffer and rise from the dead on the third day and that repentance, for the forgiveness of sins, would be preached in his name to all the nations, beginning from Jerusalem. You are witnesses of these things." Luke 24:45–48 (Year B)

This was the final appearance to the disciples as recorded in Luke's Gospel. In this appearance, Jesus showed the Apostles His hands and His feet, explained to them that He had to suffer, die and rise, as was foretold by the prophets. He exhorted them to be "witnesses of these things," He explained that very soon the Holy Spirit would come from the Father, and then walked with them to Bethany where He ascended to Heaven. These, the final earthly words of Jesus, set forth the mission of these Apostles as well as the mission of all of us.

"You are witnesses of these things," Jesus said. What things? The Apostles were to be witnesses to the Paschal Mystery: Jesus' suffering, death and Resurrection. The proclamation of these truths are the central mission of Jesus' Apostles and all of us.

How often do you think about the Paschal Mystery? Perhaps you have heard those words but do not fully understand what they are. What is the "Paschal Mystery?" The Paschal Mystery was what Jesus told the Apostles to be witnesses to. They were to be witnesses to others that Jesus came from the Father, suffered death for our sins, rose from the dead to conquer sin and then ascended into Heaven to invite us to follow. This is the most central message of our faith.

Sometimes our Christian faith can be treated more like a book of "do good lessons" than as the saving truths of our redemption. Though it's essential to understand the moral laws and the call to charitable works, we must always remember that the heart of the Gospel is about salvation. It's about Jesus dying for our sins and rising victorious so that we can enter the glories of Heaven. We do not enter Heaven simply because we are good people; rather, we are able to enter Heaven only because of the saving act of the Paschal Mystery. And though this saving act calls us to a life of charitable service to others, that charitable work is more of an effect of salvation than it is the central purpose of our faith.

The Gospel passage quoted above also says that Jesus "opened their minds to understand the Scriptures." Therefore, if we, like the Apostles, are to understand the Gospel and the central purpose of Jesus' life and our own lives, then we must allow Him to open our minds also. We must allow Jesus to reveal to us the Paschal Mystery, because it is not something we can comprehend or figure out on our own.

Reflect, today, upon how clearly you understand the purpose of the life of Christ. Do you understand the mysteries of His human life, suffering, death and Resurrection? Do you understand how these truths of our faith must change you at your very core? And do you understand your duty to be a witness to these mysteries of faith to others? Sit with these questions and allow them to sink in deeply so that you may join the Apostles in both the gift of redemption and the call to evangelize the world.

My saving Lord, Your life, death and Resurrection is the greatest gift ever given. Through this Paschal Mystery, we are set free from sin and become children of Your Father in Heaven. Open my mind to more fully understand this great gift and give me the grace I need to become Your witness to the world in need. Jesus, I trust in You.

Going All In!
Third Sunday of Easter (Year C)

> So the disciple whom Jesus loved said to Peter, "It is the Lord." When Simon Peter heard that it was the Lord, he tucked in his garment, for he was lightly clad, and jumped into the sea. John 21:7

Peter was all in, literally speaking. This passage above is taken from one of the appearances of Jesus to the Apostles after His Resurrection. They were fishing all night and caught nothing. Jesus, from the shore, told them to cast the net off the right side of the boat. When they did this they caught more fish than they could handle. When John realized it was Jesus and said so, Peter could not contain his excitement and jumped into the water to go and meet his Lord.

What a wonderful image this is to reflect upon. Specifically, it's wonderful to consider the interior excitement of Peter that led him to jump into the water and swim to the shore. His excitement could not be contained.

Would you jump into a lake to go to our Lord? That may seem like an unusual question but it's worth considering in a literal way. If you encountered our resurrected Lord, would you be so excited to see Him that you would be compelled to enter into His presence, even if it meant you had to jump into a lake? This action of Peter should be seen as a symbolic gesture for our own spiritual lives. The fact that Peter did not hesitate reveals how we should react when we encounter Jesus.

Obviously we do not encounter Jesus in His resurrected form in the way Peter did in this passage, literally and physically. But we do encounter Him every day, if we only have eyes to see. He is alive within our own hearts through prayer and by His indwelling presence. He is truly present in the people we meet every day. And He is most certainly present in the Sacraments, especially the Most Holy Eucharist.

There are two questions you should consider regarding this passage. The first is whether or not you actually do perceive Jesus' presence throughout the day. Peter did not recognize Him at first, even though Jesus spoke to him and the others in the boat. It took the miracle for them to recognize it was Him. The second question is how you react to His presence when you do perceive Him. Are you indifferent? Do you lack enthusiasm? Or are you filled with much joy?

Reflect, today, upon these two questions and resolve to become more attentive to the presence of our Lord every day, throughout the day. Resolve, also, to react as Peter did when you see Jesus. Let your heart and passion be drawn to Him and react with extraordinary joy and enthusiasm. Don't be afraid to go all in for our Lord!

Lord, help me to see You, alive in my life, alive in the lives of others, and alive in Your Church, especially in the Most Holy Eucharist. So often I am blind to Your divine presence all around me. Help me to see You every day. Help me also to respond with much joy and enthusiasm to Your divine presence. I love You, dear Lord. Help me to love You more. Jesus, I trust in You.

Seeking Jesus

Monday of the Third Week of Easter

> Jesus answered them and said, "Amen, amen, I say to you, you are looking for me not because you saw signs but because you ate the loaves and were filled. Do not work for food that perishes but for the food that endures for eternal life, which the Son of Man will give you." John 6:26–27

This Scripture goes straight to the heart of our priorities in life. What are you working for? Are you working hard for the "food that perishes" and only working slightly for the "food that endures for eternal life?" Or vice versa?

For some reason, we can easily become obsessed with working for the "things" of this world. In the passage above, people were looking for Jesus because He had fed them the day before and they were hungry again. They were looking for food, literally. Jesus gently rebukes them, taking this as an opportunity to point out the real reason they should be seeking Him. The real reason is that He wants to provide the spiritual food of eternal life. What is the food Jesus wants you to seek? That's a question you must let our Lord answer in your heart.

There are two key questions we should ponder here so as to let Him answer us. First, "What do I want in life?" Spend time with that. Spend time all by yourself and try to be honest with this question. What do you want? What is your heart's desire? If you are honest and if you let yourself face your desires you will most likely find that you have some desires, or even many, that are not put in your heart by Christ. Recognizing what these desires are is the first step to discovering what the true food is that Jesus wants to give you.

The second key question is this: "Are you seeking Jesus for the right reason?" When we are sick we seek a doctor for a cure. When a child is hurt, this child often runs to a parent for comfort. This is OK. We do the same. When we are lost and confused we often turn to God for answers and help. But, ideally, we will eventually seek God for more than just healing or comfort. We will ultimately seek God for the reason of love. We will seek Him simply because we love Him and want to love Him all the more.

Reflect, today, upon your desire to seek Jesus, or lack thereof. When you can begin to seek out Jesus simply because you love Him and want to love Him more, you are on the right road. And as you walk down that road, you find it is a road of the utmost delight and fulfillment.

Jesus, help me to seek You. Help me to seek You for the help and healing I need. But more than that, help me to seek You out of love. My Jesus, I do love You. Help me to love You more. Jesus, I trust in You.

Hunger and Thirst for the Eucharist

Tuesday of the Third Week of Easter

> Jesus said to them, "I am the bread of life; whoever comes to me will never hunger, and whoever believes in me will never thirst." John 6:35

Wouldn't it be nice if you were never hungry or thirsty again? What's fascinating is that Jesus uses these very natural human experiences to teach us about Himself. He uses natural hunger and thirst to teach us that we long to be satisfied spiritually. And there is only one way to satiate these spiritual longings…through Him.

It is a good spiritual practice to reflect upon your natural longings as an analogy for your spiritual longings. Naturally speaking, we regularly get hungry and thirsty. We eat and drink, but several hours later we hunger and thirst again.

This is a cycle we cannot avoid. Our body continually craves food and drink.

The same is true on a spiritual level. We cannot pray once and satisfy our spiritual longings forever. We cannot simply believe in Jesus and then be satisfied forever. Why? Because prayer and unity with Jesus is something that must take place daily throughout your day.

The Eucharist offers insights into this hunger and thirst in that it provides us with our "daily" food. It is a gift that we must daily seek. Some of the Sacraments are given to us only once (Baptism and Confirmation). But the Eucharist is a gift that we must continually consume and long for. The fact that we must continually go to Mass and receive the Eucharist tells us that our Christian life is not something that can be fulfilled by one definitive decision. Rather, it's something that needs daily nourishment and fulfillment.

What do you do to satisfy this Christian longing each and every day? Perhaps you cannot attend Mass every day, but do you seek to fulfill your Christian desire for Christ each and every day? Do you seek Him who is the Bread of Life every day? Do you seek to satiate your thirst with Christ each and every day?

Loving Jesus and following Him is a decision that must be renewed not only each day, it must also be renewed throughout your day. It must be renewed as often as you become physically hungry and thirsty.

Reflect, today, upon these natural longings you have for food and drink to continually remind yourself of your much deeper spiritual longing for Christ. Praying to Him, listening to Him and receiving Him into your soul is the food that satisfies like nothing else. Jesus is the true Bread of Life and your true Spiritual Drink. He is what you are made for. Let Him satisfy your deepest desires in life!

Jesus, satisfaction of my soul, I do long for You. I long to be satisfied. Help me to turn to You at all times and in all things. Help me to always remember that You are what I need and You alone satisfy. Jesus, I trust in You.

Never Rejected, Always Loved!
Wednesday of the Third Week of Easter

"I will not reject anyone who comes to me." John 6:37

This little line says much about our Lord's Divine Mercy. It is a line repeated often in St. Faustina's *Diary of Divine Mercy* and it's a statement that many people need to hear.

Why is this important to hear? Because, very often, we can carry the burden of rejection. Without even realizing it, there are many who have experienced rejection in their life and, as a result, are afraid to be vulnerable in a relationship out of fear of being hurt. Once you have been hurt in a relationship, you proceed with caution. This hurt can come from a family member, spouse, friend or anyone we've tried to reach out to in love only to receive hurt and rejection. And that hurts.

Jesus' words are especially important because they help to reassure us that Jesus is trustworthy. It is true that we can come to Him, open our hearts to Him, become completely vulnerable to Him, and He will treat us with the utmost tenderness, respect, kindness and care. Jesus will treat us with more care than we even treat ourselves!

Reflect upon these words of Jesus today. Say them over and over. "I will not reject anyone who comes to me." Know that He wants you to come to Him and to open your heart to Him completely. Doing so will allow Him to manifest His love for you and enable you to trust Him beyond what you ever imagined possible.

My welcoming Lord, I want to come to You in my sufferings and rejection. I know You are the Divine Healer and will bring comfort to my soul. Help me to trust You and to let You love me. Jesus, I trust in You.

Drawn to Jesus

Thursday of the Third Week of Easter

> Jesus said to the crowds: "No one can come to me unless the Father who sent me draw him, and I will raise him on the last day." John 6:44

This Scripture passage reveals to us a wonderful spiritual principle we need to understand and live if we are to grow close to God. It's the principle of being drawn to Jesus by the Father.

First of all, it's important to understand the first part of what Jesus says: "No one can come to me unless…" This tells us that coming to Jesus in faith, growing in that faith, and growing in our love of God is not something we can do on our own. Coming to faith is a response to God's action in our life.

This is important to understand if we wish to establish an authentic relationship with Christ because it reveals to us the fact that we have to let God take the first step in that relationship. When we let Him do this, it's our responsibility to then respond.

Of course this does not mean we just sit back in a passive way waiting for God to reach out. God is constantly reaching out, constantly speaking and constantly drawing us to Himself. So our first responsibility is to tune into His gentle "wooing." This comes in the form of gentle promptings of grace inviting us to turn more completely to Him and to surrender more fully each and every day.

In our busy world, it's so very easy to let ourselves become distracted by the many competing voices. It's easy to hear the pulling, and even pushing, of the world and all its enticements. The world has become quite good at penetrating our short attention spans and offering quick satisfactions that ultimately leave us empty.

But God's voice and His invitation are quite different. They are found in interior silence. However, we need not be in a monastery in order to achieve this interior silence. Rather, it's achieved by faithful periods of prayer each day, and a formed habit of turning to God in all things. It's achieved when we respond to God's calling, and then do it again, and again, and so forth. This builds a habit of being drawn, hearing, responding and being drawn in even closer so as to respond again.

Reflect, today, upon how well you listen to God. Try to find at least a few minutes (or more) of silence today. Close your eyes and listen. Listen to God speaking to you. When He draws you, respond to Him with much generosity. This is the best choice you can make each day!

Lord of sustaining silence, please draw me in, draw me close and help me to recognize Your voice. As I hear You calling, help me to respond to You with much generosity. My life is Yours, dear Lord. Help me to desire You all the more. Jesus, I trust in You.

The Conviction of Jesus

Friday of the Third Week of Easter

> The Jews quarreled among themselves, saying, "How can this man give us his Flesh to eat?" Jesus said to them, "Amen, amen, I say to you, unless you eat the Flesh of the Son of Man and drink his Blood, you do not have life within you." John 6:52–53

Certainly this passage reveals much about the Most Holy Eucharist, but it also reveals the strength of Jesus to speak the truth with clarity and conviction.

Jesus was facing opposition and criticism. Some were upset and challenging His words. Most of us, when we find ourselves under the scrutiny and wrath of others, will back down. We will be tempted to be overly concerned about what others say about us and about the truth we may be criticized for. But Jesus did exactly the opposite. He did not give in to the criticism of others.

It's inspiring to see that, when Jesus was faced with the harsh words of others, He responded with even greater clarity and confidence. He took His statement about the Eucharist being His Body and Blood to the next level by saying, "Amen, amen, I say to you, unless you eat the Flesh of the Son of Man and drink His Blood, you do not have life within you." This reveals a man of the utmost confidence, conviction and strength.

Of course, Jesus is God, so we should expect this from Him. But nonetheless, it is inspiring and reveals the strength we are all called to have in this world. The world we live in is filled with opposition to the truth. It's opposed to many moral truths, but it is also opposed to many of the deeper spiritual truths. These deeper truths are things such as the beautiful truths of the Eucharist, the importance of daily prayer, humility, abandonment to God, putting God's will above all things, etc. We should be aware of the fact that the closer we grow to our Lord, the more we surrender to Him, and the more we proclaim His truth, the more we will feel the pressure of the world trying to steal us away.

So what do we do? We learn from the strength and example of Jesus. Whenever we find ourselves put in a challenging position, or whenever we feel as though our faith is being attacked, we must deepen our resolve to be all the more faithful. This will make us stronger and turns those temptations we face into opportunities for grace!

Reflect, today, upon the way that you react when your faith is challenged. Do you back down, give into fear and allow the challenges from others to affect you? Or do you strengthen your resolve when challenged and allow persecution to purify your faith? Choose to imitate the strength and conviction of our Lord and you will become a greater visible instrument of His grace and mercy.

My confident Lord, give me the strength of Your conviction. Give me clarity in my mission and help me to serve You unwaveringly in all things. May I never cower when faced with the challenges of life but always deepen my resolve to serve You with all my heart. Jesus, I trust in You.

The Profound Teaching of the Holy Eucharist

Saturday of the Third Week of Easter

> As a result of this, many of his disciples returned to their former way of life and no longer walked with him. Jesus then said to the Twelve, "Do you also want to leave?" Simon Peter answered him, "Master, to whom shall we go? You have the words of eternal life." John 6:66–68

What a perfect response from Peter. The context of this story is quite fascinating and revealing. Jesus had just completed His beautiful and profound discourse on the Holy Eucharist stating clearly that His flesh is real food and His blood is real drink and that unless you eat the flesh of the Son of Man and drink His blood you have no life in you.

As a result of His teaching on the Eucharist, there were many who "returned to their former way of life and no longer walked with Him." In other words, Jesus' teaching

Third Week of Easter

on the Eucharist was difficult for many to accept and believe.

Interestingly, after Jesus speaks this profound teaching on the Eucharist, and after many leave Him as a result, He does not backpedal or change what He said. Instead, He asks His Apostles if they wish to leave also.

This question by Jesus to the Apostles is important to understand. By asking it of them in a very direct way, Jesus is giving them complete freedom to choose. He does not pressure them to believe what He just taught. This is significant because the level of detachment that Jesus offers is a way of inviting a completely free acceptance, on the part of the Apostles, of His glorious teaching on the Eucharist. They are truly free to accept or reject it. It is this freedom that allows them to radically deepen their faith in Jesus.

Peter speaks up and gives a wonderful response. "Master, to whom shall we go?" These words of Peter reveal clearly two things. First, this was a difficult situation in that people were walking away from Jesus. But secondly, Peter and the other Apostles were aware that they must believe despite the difficulty. Just because many left Jesus and refused to accept His words was no reason for the Apostles to leave Him, also. In fact, we can hear in Peter's words a manifestation of faith that they have come to believe in Jesus so completely that leaving Him would be utter foolishness. Where would they go? Why would they leave? Peter reaffirms his faith in Jesus even though following Him at that moment was not the "popular" thing to do.

Reflect, today, upon your own level of commitment to Jesus. Know that you are completely free to follow Him or to leave Him. But if you choose to follow Him, do not do it half way. Know that Jesus' words are powerful, challenging and demanding. He wants you to believe in Him and follow Him with your whole heart and with profound commitment. Jesus alone has the words of eternal life and we must accept and believe those words with all our might.

Lord, to whom else shall I go if I do not follow You? You and You alone are the One whom I choose to believe in and follow. Help me to embrace all that You have taught and help me to freely choose You each and every day of my life. Jesus, I trust in You.

Fourth Week of Easter

Christ the Good Shepherd of Us All

Fourth Sunday of Easter (Year A)—Good Shepherd Sunday

> "But whoever enters through the gate is the shepherd of the sheep. The gatekeeper opens it for him, and the sheep hear his voice, as the shepherd calls his own sheep by name and leads them out. " John 10:2–4

Four things happen in this story:

> First, the gatekeeper opens the gate for the shepherd.
> Second, the shepherd calls his own sheep by name.
> Third, the sheep hear his voice.
> Fourth, the shepherd leads the sheep through the gate.

Who is the "gatekeeper?" Saint Augustine says that one answer to this is that the gatekeeper is the Holy Spirit. The role of the Holy Spirit is to open our minds to the truth, to a deeper understanding of Scripture, and therefore, to a deeper understanding of Christ Himself. Therefore, the Holy Spirit will open your mind and your heart to know and love Christ as your shepherd, if you let Him.

Once this happens, Jesus, the Good Shepherd, will speak your name, personally. Not audibly, but through the gift of faith. You are not only one of many sheep; rather, you are His dear one whom He knows and loves on an intimate and personal level. Therefore, this passage calls us to an intimate and personal relationship with Christ the Good Shepherd.

Knowing we are personally and intimately loved by Christ, that we are called by name, invites and encourages us to listen. Do you listen? And if you listen, do you hear? "Hearing" Christ speak to us in this personal and intimate way should motivate us to action.

What action? To be led. Normally a shepherd walks behind the sheep and they run on ahead. But in this story, Jesus, the Good Shepherd, Who calls you by name, leads you "through the gate." Jesus Himself is the Gate. We are called to become one with Him and, through Him, to enter into the bosom of the Father in Heaven. Through Him we enter into new life itself, life of union with Him Who is our Shepherd.

Reflect, today, upon this fourfold journey to which you are called. Pray to the Holy Spirit that your mind and heart will be opened to know and love Christ. Then prayerfully listen for Christ to speak to you. Hear Him, respond to Him and allow Him to draw you into His open heart of perfect love.

Holy Spirit, please open my ears to the Voice of the Good Shepherd and my mind to all that He speaks. My precious Lord Jesus, You are my Shepherd, I choose, this day, to follow Your voice when You speak, and to do so with complete trust and abandon. I love You, my Lord, and I thank you for loving me with such tender and intimate care. Jesus, my Good Shepherd, I trust in You.

Laying Down Your Life

Fourth Sunday of Easter (Year B)—Good Shepherd Sunday

> Jesus said: "I am the good shepherd. A good shepherd lays down his life for the sheep. A hired man, who is not a shepherd and whose sheep are not his own, sees a wolf coming and leaves the sheep and runs away, and the wolf catches and scatters them. This is because he works for pay and has no concern for the sheep." John 10:11

Traditionally, this Fourth Sunday of Easter is called "Good Shepherd Sunday." This is because the readings for this Sunday from all three liturgical years come from the tenth chapter of John's Gospel in which Jesus teaches clearly and repeatedly about His role of being the Good Shepherd. What does it mean to be a shepherd? More specifically, how is it that Jesus most perfectly acts as the Good Shepherd of us all?

The image of Jesus being a shepherd is an endearing image. Many artists have shown Jesus as a gentle and kind man holding a sheep in His arms or on His shoulders. In part, it is this holy image that we put before our mind's eye to ponder today. This is an inviting image and one that helps us to turn to our Lord, as a child would turn to a parent in need. But though this gentle and endearing image of Jesus as a shepherd is quite inviting, there are other aspects of His role as Shepherd that should also be considered.

The Gospel quoted above gives us the heart of Jesus' definition of the most important quality of a good shepherd. He is one who "lays down his life for the sheep." He is one who is willing to suffer, out of love, for those entrusted to his care. He is one who chooses the life of the sheep over his own life. At the heart of this teaching is sacrifice. A shepherd is sacrificial. And being sacrificial is the truest and most accurate definition of love.

Though Jesus is the "Good Shepherd" Who gave His life for us all, we must also daily strive to imitate His sacrificial love for others. We must be Christ, the Good Shepherd, to others every day. And the way we do this is by looking for ways to lay our lives down for others, putting them first, overcoming every selfish tendency, and serving them with our lives. Love is not only experiencing endearing and heartwarming moments with others; first and foremost, love is about being sacrificial.

Reflect, today, upon these two images of Jesus the Good Shepherd. First, ponder the tender and gentle Lord Who welcomes you and cares for you in a holy, compassionate, and endearing way. But then turn your eyes to the Crucifixion. Our Good Shepherd did, indeed, give His life for us all. His shepherding love led Him to suffer greatly and to lay His life down so that we could be saved. Jesus was not afraid to die for us, because His love was perfect. We are the ones who matter to Him, and He was willing to do anything necessary to love us, including sacrificing His life out of love. Ponder this most holy and pure sacrificial love and strive to more fully offer this same love to all those whom you are called to love.

Jesus our Good Shepherd, I thank You profoundly for loving me to the point of sacrificing Your life on the Cross. You love me not only with the utmost tenderness and compassion but also in a sacrificial and selfless way. As I receive Your divine love, dear Lord, help me to also imitate Your love and to sacrifice my life for others. Jesus, my Good Shepherd, I trust in You.

Contrasting Voices

Fourth Sunday of Easter (Year C)—Good Shepherd Sunday

"My sheep hear my voice; I know them, and they follow me." John 10:27

Jesus offers a clear contrast among shepherds. This would apply to priests, parents and all of us in our own unique way. The contrast He offers is between the ones who care deeply for those entrusted to their care, and those who are just going through the motions and are more motivated by selfishness than sacrificial love.

Jesus perfectly manifested sacrificial love as the Divine Shepherd. He was willing to go all the way for us, His sheep. He was willing to sacrifice everything. He did not let suffering, persecution, rejection and the like deter Him from His responsibility of caring for us in a total and complete way. It should inspire us, console us and encourage us to know how deep His love for us really is.

This love is seen, also, in the unwavering love of a parent, sibling, or dear friend. When the love one offers us is unwavering, especially in difficult times, this is a great support. And love offered to another like this forges a deep spiritual bond that is stronger than any hardship we may face. No matter what "wolf" comes our way, we must know of the unwavering support of the Divine Shepherd. And when we can see that love made manifest in the unwavering support of others, we are doubly blessed.

But the contrast should not be ignored either. Jesus gives the example of "a hired man who is not a shepherd" who sees the wolf coming and runs. It's important to point out how damaging this man is to the people of God. When he runs from his responsibility and gives into selfish motivation, he leaves the flock untended and vulnerable to attack.

We should see in this hired man the temptation we all inevitably face in life. It's hard to stick with it through the hard times. It's hard to be there for those who need us when they need us. It's hard to be faithful in all things and to never shy away in the face of the temptation of fear.

Jesus offers His unwavering love and support to us as our Shepherd, but He also wants us to return this gift to Him by offering this same unwavering commitment to one another.

Reflect, today, how well you imitate the Good Shepherd. Where you are lacking, let Him shepherd you so that you may shepherd others. Run to the Good Shepherd and trust in His perfect love for you.

Jesus, our Good Shepherd, I thank You for Your unwavering support of me as my Shepherd. And I thank You for those who act as Your instruments of this deep love and commitment. Help me to fulfill my role of shepherding Your people, the people You have placed in my life.

May I never run from the glorious responsibility You have called me to. Jesus, I trust in You.

The Voice of the Shepherd

Monday of the Fourth Week of Easter

Note: In year A, when this Gospel is read on the previous Sunday, John 10:11–18 is used today.

> "...the sheep hear his voice, as he calls his own sheep by name and leads them out. When he has driven out all his own, he walks ahead of them, and the sheep follow him, because they recognize his voice. But they will not follow a stranger; they will run away from him, because they do not recognize the voice of strangers." John 10:3–5

What are you most familiar with in life? What voice or voices echo in your mind most of the time? There are many influences we receive on a regular basis. Some are good and some are not so good. Oftentimes we can talk ourselves into believing that the many "voices" or influences that we encounter on a daily basis do not affect us. We are pressured by the voice of the media, pop culture, love of money, a desire for recognition and so much more. These are powerful influences and, whether we want to believe it or not, they do affect us.

The Gospel above gives us insight into this internal struggle in that it contrasts the voice of the Shepherd with the voice of a stranger. The sheep are easily taught and conditioned. They learn the voice of their shepherd because it was common practice for shepherds to regularly speak to their sheep. Once the sheep became used to the shepherd's voice, they would turn and follow him when he called.

So it is with us. We will follow the voice of that which we are most familiar with. Whatever it is that we immerse ourselves in each and every day will grow on us and draw us, even unknowingly, to follow.

This begs the question, "What are you most familiar with?" Ideally, we spend sufficient time in God's Word, learning His language, tone and voice. Ideally, we dedicate some portion of our day, every day, to silent contemplation of God. As we do this, we build a habit of hearing Him speak and we become comfortable with and comforted by His voice.

Once this habit is established in us, it will be much easier to go about our busy day hearing God whenever He chooses to speak. We will immediately recognize it is Him and we will follow.

Reflect, today, upon that which calls to you the loudest. Don't let the many other voices in our world drown out God's voice. Instead, prepare yourself for the moments He chooses to speak. And when He does speak, let that voice grab your attention so that you can follow.

My speaking Lord, help me to know and love Your gentle voice throughout my daily life. May that voice overwhelm all others that compete for my attention. I choose You, dear Lord, as my one Shepherd and guide. Jesus, I trust in You.

The Language of Jesus

Tuesday of the Fourth Week of Easter

> Jesus walked about in the temple area on the Portico of Solomon. So the Jews gathered around him and said to him, "How long are you going to keep us in suspense? If you are the Christ, tell us plainly." Jesus answered them, "I told you and you do not believe." John 10:24–25

This statement of Jesus may have left His followers confused. They wanted to believe that Jesus was the Messiah, and so they asked Him to tell them plainly if He was the Messiah. And how did He respond? He tells them that He already told them and they failed to believe. This is an interesting situation.

The first thing to say about this is that Jesus was not being critical. He was helping them to understand His language. He was helping them to understand that the answer to their question was not a matter of Jesus simply telling them, "I am the Messiah!" Rather, the answer to their question had to come to them from the Father in Heaven, spoken to their hearts as they listened to Jesus and witnessed His miracles. The answer was to be given to them by the gift of faith that had to be received from within. This gift of faith would give them the certainty they so desired.

The same is true with us. Perhaps you've wanted God to come down from Heaven at times and tell you "plainly" the answer to this or that question. But He does not do that. He does it in His perfect way with His perfect language. It's the language of faith and it requires a complete submission of our minds and wills to God to hear and understand. This is the only way to become converted in the way God wants us to be.

Reflect, today, on how well you listen to God speak. You most likely can learn to listen to Him more clearly, discerning His voice of Truth. As you hear Him, let yourself become completely convinced of all that He says. And let that deep conviction rule your life.

Lord of all Truth, I so often do not let myself hear You plainly through the gift of faith. I so often want the easy answer to the difficult questions. Help me to grow in patience so that I may know You and allow You to become my true Shepherd. Jesus, I trust in You.

Evangelizing Through Unity

Wednesday of the Fourth Week of Easter

> Jesus cried out and said, "Whoever believes in me believes not only in me but also in the one who sent me, and whoever sees me sees the one who sent me." John 12:44–45

Now on a literal level, this is hard to comprehend. How is it that those who looked at Jesus were looking also at the Father? How is it that seeing Jesus was seeing the Father in Heaven?

The answer is quite simple. The unity that the Father and the Son share is a perfect unity. They remain distinct Persons but they are also united as one. They are united in their perfect love and in the perfect communion of their wills.

For that reason, knowing Jesus is also knowing the Father. But the truth is that the Father's presence is veiled just as the divinity of the Son is veiled. Though we do not have the experience of seeing Jesus walk the Earth as the first disciples did, we find the same reality every time we come before the Holy Eucharist. When we enter a church and genuflect before the tabernacle, it's important to always be exceptionally cognizant of the fact that we are in the full divine presence of God the Son. And for that reason, we are also in the full and divine presence of the Father! Their presence is real and absolute. It's just that they are hidden from our five senses.

But one key thing to ponder here is the unity of the Father, the Son and the Holy Spirit. Prayerfully reflecting upon their unity is a very healthy meditation for our prayer life. Why? Because we are called to share in Their unity, and we are called to share in unity with one another.

Unity is hard. It takes a tremendous amount of love. It means being fully present to the other, seeking to fully understand, accept and know them. And the Trinity is our model for this. Be it parents and children, spouses, friends or others, we are called to a deep and abiding unity.

Think about someone you know well. And think about someone that person knows well and loves. To a certain degree, you may feel you know that other person just by knowing the one who knows them. For example, say you have a very close friend who has a child and your friend shares much with you about their child. What you're experiencing is the unity of that parent and child in your relationship with your friend.

So it is with God. As we come to know God the Son, we automatically come to know God the Father. And the good news is that if we know God, and then let another get to know us, the effect is that we will be letting them come to know God through us. This is one of the wonderful ways to evangelize and bring God to those whom we know and love.

Reflect, today, upon your relationship with God and how that relationship shines through in all other relationships you have. Commit yourself more fully to knowing and loving God so that others around you may also benefit from your love of Him.

Lord of perfect unity, help me to come to know and love You and, in that relationship, to come to know and love the Father and the Holy Spirit. And as I grow in love for You Most Holy Trinity, help me to bring that love into every relationship I have so that I may be an instrument of Your love to others. Most Holy Trinity, I trust in You.

Slaves of Christ

Thursday of the Fourth Week of Easter

> When Jesus had washed the disciples' feet, he said to them: "Amen, amen, I say to you, no slave is greater than his master nor any messenger greater than the one who sent him." John 13:16

If we read between the lines we can hear Jesus telling us two things. First, that it's good to see ourselves as slaves and messengers of God, and second, that we are to always give the glory to God. These are important points to live in the spiritual life. Let's look at both.

Normally, the idea of being a "slave" is not all that desirable. We are not as familiar with slavery in our day and age, but it is real and has caused extreme damage throughout the history of our world in many cultures and at many times. The worst part about slavery is the cruelty with which the slaves are treated. They are treated as objects and property which is completely contrary to their human dignity.

But imagine the scenario where a person is a slave to one who loves him perfectly and has as his primary mission to help that "slave" realize his true potential and fulfillment in life. In this case, the master would "command" the slave to embrace love and happiness and would never violate his human dignity.

This is the way it is with God. We should never fear the idea of being a slave of God. Though this language may carry baggage from abuses of human dignity of the past, slavery to God should be our goal. Why? Because God is the one we should want as our master. In fact, we should desire God as our master even more than we desire to be our own master. God will treat us better than we treat ourselves! He will dictate to us a perfect life of holiness and happiness and we will be humbly submissive to His divine will. And what's more, He will give us the necessary means to achieve all that

He dictates to us if we let Him. Being a "slave of God" is a good thing and should be our goal in life.

As we grow in our ability to let God take control of our life, we must also regularly enter into an attitude of thanks and praise of God for all that He does in us. We must point all the glory to Him for letting us share in His mission and for being sent by Him to fulfill His will. He is greater in every way, but He also wants us to share in that greatness and glory. So, the good news is that when we glorify and thank God for all He does in us and for all the dictates of His law and His commands, we will be elevated by God to participate in and share in His glory! This is one fruit of the Christian life that blesses us beyond what we could ever come up with ourselves.

Reflect, today, upon letting yourself become a complete slave of God and His will today. That commitment will start you down a path of tremendous delight.

My Lord and Master, I submit myself to Your every command. May Your will be done in me and only Your will. I choose You as my Master in all things and trust in Your perfect love for me. Jesus, I trust in You.

Our Father's House

Friday of the Fourth Week of Easter

> "In my Father's house there are many dwelling places. If there were not, would I have told you that I am going to prepare a place for you? And if I go and prepare a place for you, I will come back again and take you to myself, so that where I am you also may be." John 14:2–3

From time to time it's important that we focus in on the glorious reality of Heaven! Heaven is real and, God willing,

Fourth Week of Easter

one day we will all be united there with our Triune God. If we properly understood Heaven, we'd long for it with a deep and burning love and we'd look forward to it with a powerful desire, being filled with peace and joy every time we think of it.

Unfortunately, however, the thought of leaving this Earth and meeting our Maker is a frightening thought for some. Perhaps it's the fear of the unknown, the realization that we will leave our loved ones behind, or possibly even a fear that Heaven will not be our final resting place.

As Christians, it's essential that we work at fostering a great love of Heaven by gaining a proper understanding of not only Heaven itself, but also the purpose of our lives on Earth. Heaven helps order our lives and helps us stay on the path that leads to this eternal beatitude.

In the passage above, we are given a very consoling image of Heaven. It's the image of the "Father's house." This image is a good one to reflect upon because it reveals that Heaven is our home. Home is a safe place. It's a place where we can be ourselves, relax, be with loved ones, and feel as if we belong. We are God's sons and daughters and He has decided that we belong there with Him.

Reflecting on this image of Heaven should also console those who have lost a loved one. The experience of saying goodbye, for now, is very difficult. And it should be difficult. The difficulty of losing a loved one reveals that there is true love in that relationship. And that is good. But God does want the feelings of loss to also be mingled with joy as we ponder the reality of our loved one being with the Father in His home for eternity. They are happier there than we will ever be able to imagine, and we will one day be called to share in that joy.

Reflect, today, upon this image of Heaven: our Father's House. Sit with that image and let God speak to you. As you do, let your heart be drawn to Heaven so that this desire will help to direct your actions here and now.

Lord of Heaven and Earth, I do long to be with You eternally in Heaven. I long to be comforted, consoled and filled with joy in Your home. Help me to always keep this as my goal in life and to grow, daily in a desire for this final resting place. Jesus, I trust in You.

Speaking With Confidence
Saturday of the Fourth Week of Easter

"The words that I speak to you I do not speak on my own." John 14:10

These words from Jesus, once again, reveal the intimate unity He has with His Father. He and the Father are one and what He says also comes from the Father. John's Gospel is filled with this language as a way of highlighting their perfect unity.

Though there is much we could say about the unity of the Father and the Son, it's important to remind ourselves that these words spoken by Jesus should also ideally be words we speak. How wonderful it is to be able to say that WE also do not speak on our own but that the Father speaks through us. This should be our constant goal.

If we speak words to others on our own, relying upon our own wisdom and insights, then we must also humbly admit that our words will not be that powerful. This is hard to admit but is true. We can easily fall into the trap of thinking our opinions are right and that others need to listen to us.

If, on the other hand, we are able to speak words that have the backing of the Father, words that are spoken from His heart, then we will begin to see that those words make a true difference in the lives of others. Words matter and we should always be very careful as to what we say and how we say it.

Allowing the Father to speak in and through us suddenly gives our words new conviction and power. They become words that God speaks to others and words that enable God to make a difference in their lives.

Reflect, today, upon your daily speech. If you struggle with not knowing what to say, or how to say it at times, then a good prayer to pray is for the grace to speak only that which the Father gives you to speak; nothing more and nothing less. Pray that prayer and be confident that God has a lot to say through you.

Father in Heaven, give me Your words to speak. Help me to always turn to You in my heart in confidence so that You are the source of all truth and goodness. May that truth and goodness come forth from me each and every day. Jesus, I trust in You.

Fifth Week of Easter

The Only Way to Salvation

Fifth Sunday of Easter (Year A)

> "I am the way and the truth and the life. No one comes to the Father except through me." John 14:6

Are you saved? Hopefully the answer to this is "Yes" in three ways: You were saved by grace through Baptism, you continue to be saved by God's grace and mercy as you freely choose to follow Him, and you hope to be saved in your final hour so as to enter the glories of Heaven. Anything we accomplish in life means nothing if we cannot answer "Yes" in this threefold way.

It's also important to be reminded of how we are saved. How is it that we were, are and hope to receive the precious gift of salvation? The answer is simple: Through the life, death and Resurrection of Jesus Christ, our one and only Way to the Father. There is no other way we obtain salvation than through Him.

Sometimes we can fall into the trap of thinking that we achieve salvation by simply being "good." In other words, do your good works save you? The proper answer is both "Yes" and "No." It is "Yes" only in the sense that our good works are a necessary part of union with Christ. Without Him we can do nothing good. But if we have accepted Christ into our life and, thus, if we are on the road to salvation, then good works will be necessarily present in our life. But the answer is also "No" in the sense that Jesus and Jesus alone is the only Savior. We cannot save ourselves no matter how hard we try to be good.

This discussion is especially familiar among our evangelical Christian brothers and sisters. But it's a conversation we should be quite familiar with also. At the heart of this conversation is the Person of Jesus Christ. He and He alone must be the central focus of our lives and we must see Him as the Way, the Truth and the Life. He is the only Way to Heaven, He is the fullness of the Truth we must believe, and He is the Life that we are called to live and is the source of this new life of Grace.

Reflect, today, upon the central and singular role of Jesus in your life. Without Him you are nothing, but with Him you obtain the life of perfect fulfillment. Choose Him in a very personal and concrete way this day as your Lord and Savior. Humbly admit that you are nothing without Him and let Him into your life so that He can offer you to His loving Father in Heaven.

My Lord and my Savior, I say "Yes" to You this day and accept You into my life as my Lord and Savior. I thank You for the gift of Baptism which began my life of grace and I renew my choice to follow You, this day, so that You may enter more fully into my life. As You enter into my life, please offer me to the Father in Heaven. May all my actions be directed by You so that I may be an eternal offering with You, dear Jesus. Jesus, I trust in You.

Humility and Gratitude

Fifth Sunday of Easter (Year B)

> "I am the vine, you are the branches. Whoever remains in me and I in him will bear much fruit, because without me you can do nothing." John 15:5

What a great little reminder... "Without me you can do nothing."

At first, hearing this may hurt. It may hurt our pride and we may react to this idea negatively. Is it really true? Can we really do nothing without God? Obviously the answer to that is "Yes." Jesus does not lie. We can do nothing without God in our lives.

In fact, if God were to forget us for one moment, we would cease to exist. Even our very existence depends upon God continuing to will that we exist. And as for doing good, making a difference, having a productive life, etc., we can do nothing good without God's grace.

Though this may be hard to hear at first, we should ponder it regularly. And if we do ponder it and embrace this truth, two things will happen in our souls. First, we will grow in humility. Humility is the most important virtue in which we can grow. It's been referred to as "the mother of all virtues." This is because from this virtue all other virtues flow. Humility means we realize that God is everything and that we need Him with a 100% need. This humble truth will enable us to seek God in all things and invite Him deeply into every part of our lives.

A second thing that will happen in our souls when we realize that we can do nothing without God is that we will grow in gratitude. As we see that God is everything AND we begin to see that He provides us with constant grace in our lives, our only appropriate response will be "Thank you!" We will be grateful to God for everything because we will realize that everything that is good is a gift from Him.

Reflect, today, upon these truths of humility and gratitude and allow them to sink in. As you do, allow these virtues to grow to greater fruition in your life.

My God and my All, I do believe that I can do nothing without You. Help me to believe this with an even greater conviction and, as I do, help me to grow in humility and gratitude. Jesus, I trust in You.

Glorification Through Suffering

Fifth Sunday of Easter (Year C)

> When Judas had left them, Jesus said, "Now is the Son of Man glorified, and God is glorified in him." John 13:31

It is essential to know the end of the story. Jesus knew the end when He spoke these words to the Apostles at the Last Supper right after Judas left to go and betray Him. It's important to put this situation within the context that Jesus understood it. From a purely human point of view, one of Jesus' closest friends was about to betray Him for money. For most of us this would have been devastating and the cause for anger and hurt. But because Jesus knew the end of the story, He was able to see Judas' betrayal as the means to His glorification, not His defeat. He turned His eyes toward Heaven and all that He would accomplish through His suffering rather than look at the immediate pain He would soon endure.

This is a powerful lesson for us all. First, it's essential that we look at Jesus' glorification through His betrayal, suffering and death. But we must also strive to see the potential that our own sufferings have when united to the Savior of the World.

How do you react when another sins against you? How would you have reacted to Judas betraying your love? This is a very difficult question to face in honesty and it is even harder to live the response that Jesus lived. The truth is that every time we are mistreated by another, we are given an opportunity to glorify God and further the Kingdom of Heaven by forgiving, uniting our suffering with Christ's, and offering mercy. This is much easier to speak about than to live.

Reflect, today, upon this scene of the Gospel. Gaze upon Judas leaving the Last Supper and going out into the night to betray our Lord. But look at it in the way Jesus saw it. Look at it with the understanding that this was the means chosen by the Father to bring salvation to the world. Reflect, also, upon every opportunity that you are given to do as Jesus did. Try to be concrete and specific and see any and every suffering you endure as a glorious opportunity to dispense the mercy of God. Though this may be difficult at first, it is this act of love that will give great glory to the Father in Heaven!

My dear Lord, You were betrayed by the kiss of one of Your closest friends. But in Your perfect wisdom, You saw this betrayal as the perfect opportunity to glorify the Father through Your mercy and forgiveness. Lord, I also have betrayed You countless times. For that reason I am sorry. But I thank You for loving me and forgiving me with Your Heart of perfect mercy. Help me to receive that mercy and to offer it to others who have sinned against me. Jesus, I trust in You.

Indwelling of the Trinity

Monday of the Fifth Week of Easter

> "Whoever loves me will keep my word, and my Father will love him, and we will come to him and make our dwelling with him." John 14:23

Children seem to get it. They seem to understand that God dwells in their hearts. Of course if you asked them how they know this they may look at you with a confused look and not know how to respond. But, nonetheless, somehow they do understand that God dwells within them.

So what would you say if someone asked you, "How do you know that God comes and makes His dwelling within you?" Perhaps you also may be at a loss for words to describe this incredible mystery of our faith. Do you believe this to be true? That God wants to make your heart and soul His dwelling place? If so, how does this happen?

By the gift of faith we, like little children, just know that God wants to dwell within us. We know that He wants to possess our souls, speak to us, strengthen us, lead us and guide us. We know, by the gift of faith, that God is real and desires the deepest and most intimate relationship with us. We just know.

The good news is that faith leads to understanding. This means that the more we are attentive to the voice of God speaking within us, leading and guiding us, the more we begin to understand His indwelling presence. As St. Augustine said, "Faith is to believe what you do not see. The reward of faith is to see what you believe." Faith in God's indwelling presence leads us to the answer of the question above. The answer is one that God and God alone can give to us. We can share our faith with others, give witness to His presence in our lives, and give those around us the answer to that question through faith. How do I know God dwells within me? The answer: Because I see Him there, I speak to Him there, and He speaks to me.

Reflect, today, upon the Lord living within you. Let Him speak to you and, in that ever deepening conversation, allow His Indwelling Presence to grow and to become manifest to others. God wants to not only dwell within you, He also wants to shine through you.

Most Blessed Trinity, come live in my heart. Make my heart Your dwelling place. Help me to see You there, to meet You there, to converse with You and to love You in my soul. Jesus, I trust in You.

A Troubled Heart

Tuesday of the Fifth Week of Easter

"Do not let your hearts be troubled or afraid." John 14:27

What a wonderful reminder that we all need to hear on a regular basis. "Do not let your heart be troubled." And "Do not let your heart be afraid." How often do you follow that advice?

Interestingly, it's actually more than advice. It's a command of love from our Lord. He wants to be clear and wants us to know that a fearful and troubled heart is not of Him. To be troubled and fearful is a great burden and weighs us down. Jesus desperately wants us to be free of these burdens. He wants us to be free so that we can experience the joy of life.

So what is it that burdens you in life the most? Is there something in your life that you obsess about, are angry about, can't let go of or that tends to dominate your life? Or perhaps your burden is more subtle. Perhaps there is nothing that overwhelms you but, instead, is a constant burden in a small way, always there in the background. These burdens can be quite difficult when they last from year to year.

The first step to freedom is to see the burden for what it is. Identify it and seek to identify the underlying cause. If the cause of your burden is your own sin, repent of it and seek Confession. This is the best way to experience immediate freedom.

If, however, your burden is the result of another's actions or some situation in life that is out of your control, then you are in a unique position to surrender to our Lord, giving Him complete control of this situation. Freedom is found in total surrender, trust and abandonment to His will.

Spend some time today reflecting upon that which burdens you the most in life. What is it that weighs heavily upon you? It is this, more than anything else, that Jesus wants to enter into and lift for you. He wants you free so that you can experience the joy that He has to offer you in life.

Lord of true joy, I want to be free. I want to experience the joy You have in store for me. When the burdens of life weigh me down, help me to turn to You in my need. Jesus, I trust in You.

Being Pruned

Wednesday of the Fifth Week of Easter

"I am the true vine, and my Father is the vine grower. He takes away every branch in me that does not bear fruit, and everyone that does he prunes so that it bears more fruit." John 15:1–2

Are you willing to let yourself be pruned? Pruning is necessary if a plant is to produce an abundance of good fruit or beautiful flowers. If, for example, a grapevine is left to grow without pruning, it will produce many small grapes that are good for nothing. But if care is taken to prune the vine, the maximum number of good grapes will be produced.

Jesus uses this image of pruning to teach us a similar lesson in bearing good fruit for His Kingdom. He wants our lives to be fruitful and He wants to use us as powerful instruments of His grace in the world. But unless we are willing to go through the purification of spiritual pruning from time to time, we will not be the instruments that God can use.

Spiritual pruning takes the form of letting God eliminate the vices in our lives so that the virtues can be properly nourished. This is especially done by letting Him humble us and strip away our pride. This can hurt, but the pain associated with being humbled by God is a key to spiritual growth. By growing in humility, we grow ever more reliant upon the source of our nourishment rather than relying upon ourselves, our own ideas and our own plans. God is infinitely wiser than us and if we can continually turn to Him as our source, we will be far stronger and better prepared to let Him do great things through us. But, again, this requires that we let Him prune us.

Being spiritually pruned means we actively let go of our own will and our own ideas. It means we give up control over our lives and let the master grower take over. It means we trust Him far more than we trust ourselves. This requires a true death to ourselves and a true humility by which we acknowledge we are completely reliant upon God in the same way a branch is reliant upon the vine. Without the vine, we shrivel and die. Being firmly attached to the vine is the only way to life.

Pray this day that you will let the Lord prune away all that is not of Him in your life. Trust in Him and His divine plan and know that this is the only path to bearing the good fruit God wants to bear through you.

Lord, I pray that You prune away all my pride and selfishness. Purify me of my many sins so that I can turn to You in all things. And as I learn to rely upon You, may You begin to bear an abundance of good fruit in my life. Jesus, I trust in You.

Unlimited and Unconditional Love

Thursday of the Fifth Week of Easter

"As the Father loves me, so I also love you." John 15:9

There are three beautiful insights we should take from this passage.

First, the love of the Father for the Son is perfect in every way. It is unconditional and all-consuming. It's total and selfless. In receiving the Father's love, Jesus receives all He needs.

Second, the love Jesus receives from the Father cannot be contained. It cannot be kept to Himself. The love of the Father is such that it overflows from Jesus' heart. It is this overflowing love that pours forth from Jesus to us.

Third, a key thing to ponder in this is that this overflowing love, now given to us, cannot be contained within us either. It must overflow from our hearts to others. Therefore, if we are to be true recipients of the love of the Father and the Son, we must in turn let that love pour forth onto others in an "unlimited" and "unconditional" way.

Think about it. "Unlimited." "Unconditional." Is this truly possible? Is it possible to be so radical and total in our love of others? Yes, it's possible only if the love we speak of originates in the heart of the Father, given to the Son, and then poured out upon us to distribute freely.

Reflect, today, upon the fact that the love you are called to share with others originates in the Heart of the Father in Heaven. The first and most important step in learning to love with the Father's Heart is to let God love you. This can be very hard to do. It can be hard to let God love you, to receive that love, and to let it affect you deeply. But if you can continually let God love you with His perfect love, you will start to see that this love automatically flows forth from you as if it were an overflowing river of grace and mercy.

Loving Father and Son, I do love You and know that I am loved by You. Help me to be open to Your love. Help me to let that love sink in so that it may also overflow from my heart to others. Jesus, I trust in You.

You Are Chosen
Friday of the Fifth Week of Easter

> "It was not you who chose me, but I who chose you and appointed you to go and bear fruit that will remain." John 15:16

Children love to play games. When a game is organized between two teams, kids will often line up and wait to be chosen. Each child hopes to be chosen first. It is affirming to be wanted for the team. When a child is chosen last this can be difficult and hurtful.

This reveals the desire within each of us to belong and to be wanted. The good news is that God does choose each one of us. He wants us as a member of His family and He wants us to belong to Him. This is essential to understand and, when it is understood, it is very affirming.

It is a good spiritual practice to regularly reflect upon the fact that God chose us even before we were born. He knew us from all eternity and set His eyes upon us, longing to bring us into His fold. We need to understand this, accept it and believe it. We do belong.

God not only chooses us to belong to Him, He also chooses us for His mission. He wants to use us to go and bear fruit for His Kingdom. He wants to use us for a sacred purpose and a divine calling. Being a member of His "team" means that our lives have purpose and meaning. No matter how "unqualified" we may feel at times to make a difference, we must remember that God does not see us that way. Rather, He sees the infinite potential within each of us and chooses to use that potential for the building up of His Kingdom.

Reflect, this day, on two short phrases: "I have chosen you" and "Go and bear fruit." Accepting your call from God will change your life and will also change the lives of those whom you are called to serve.

My welcoming Lord, I know You have chosen me. I accept Your call in my life. I accept the fact that You have appointed me to fulfill Your mission in a unique and glorious way. Help me to continually say "Yes" to Your call. Jesus, I trust in You.

Persecution

Saturday of the Fifth Week of Easter

> "Remember the word I spoke to you, 'No slave is greater than his master.' If they persecuted me, they will also persecute you." John 15:20

Do you want to be like Jesus? If so, beware of what that means. It's easy to think that the closer we grow to Christ the more we will be loved and understood by the world. We can think that everyone will see our holiness and admire it and all will be good and easy in life.

But all we have to do is look at the life of Christ to know this is not the case. He was obviously perfect in every way. As a result, He was treated with great malice and persecution. It's hard to fathom the dark truth that they actually killed Him. In the dark of the night, He was arrested, given a mock trial, found guilty and sentenced to death. His punishment was then carried out immediately.

Fifth Week of Easter

Why did they do this to the Son of God? Why would someone so perfect and merciful in every way be so cruelly treated?

If we were there, as His first followers, we would have most likely been shocked, frightened, scandalized and confused. We may have thought that Jesus messed up and lost hope in Him. But His plan was perfect in every way and His plan did centrally involve Him enduring false accusations and malicious persecution. And by freely accepting this abuse, He redeemed the world.

So back to the original question, "Do you want to be like Jesus?" This is a tough question when we look at it in the light of what happened to Him. "No slave is greater than his master." "If they persecuted me, they will also persecute you." These are tough sayings to accept and agree to.

Persecution is something from which we should not run. We should not despair if it happens and we should not hold our head low. Why? Because persecution is a clear sign that we are following in the footsteps of our Master. We are more deeply united to Christ as a result of persecution than we could ever realize.

The key is to know that God intends to use all maltreatment for good if we let Him. And we let Him use it for good when we surrender it to Him and receive it freely, not begrudgingly. Our response must be to "rejoice and be glad" that we have been found worthy to follow in the steps of our Divine Lord.

Ponder today any form of persecution or injustice you suffer for the sake of your faith and embrace of the Gospel. The Lord wants to use that if you let Him.

My persecuted Lord, I do surrender to You all that weighs me down. I give any suffering I receive for being Your follower. May I not only imitate You in Your suffering, but also in Your willing embrace of it. Jesus, I trust in You.

Sixth Week of Easter

The Coming of the Spirit of Truth

Sixth Sunday of Easter (Year A)

> "If you love me, you will keep my commandments. And I will ask the Father, and he will give you another Advocate to be with you always, the Spirit of truth, whom the world cannot accept…" John 14:15–17

On this, the Sixth Sunday of Easter, we begin to turn our eyes toward the coming of the Holy Spirit. In this passage above, Jesus speaks of asking the Father to send another Advocate to be with us always. This Advocate is the Holy Spirit.

Interestingly, Jesus uses the title, "Spirit of Truth" to refer to the Holy Spirit. He also points out that the world cannot accept the Holy Spirit.

We are currently living in what we may call the "Age of the Holy Spirit." This is the age that Jesus spoke about with His Apostles. Therefore, it's good to look at the coming of the Holy Spirit in the way Jesus revealed it.

First, regarding the title, "Spirit of Truth," we should ponder whether we are able and willing to accept the full Truth that comes with receiving the Holy Spirit. If we are of the world, embracing worldly ideas and values, then we will not be able to accept the Holy Spirit. However, if we are able to see the errors of our world and the many false values within it, we will more easily be able to reject those values and embrace the Holy Spirit and the many truths that the Spirit reveals.

Furthermore, if we are open to the coming of the Holy Spirit, we will receive the greatest Advocate we can have in life. The Holy Spirit is THE Advocate, meaning, the only helper we need. Becoming consumed by the Holy Spirit provides us with every grace necessary in life.

Reflect, today, upon the fact that Jesus' promise to His Apostles has been fulfilled and that you have the ability to receive that promise here and now in your life. Say a prayer to the Holy Spirit and anticipate celebrating Pentecost Sunday in two weeks.

Come Holy Spirit, fill the hearts of your faithful and kindle in them the fire of Your love. Send forth Your Spirit and they shall be created. And You shall renew the face of the earth.

O, God, who by the light of the Holy Spirit, did instruct the hearts of the faithful, grant that by the same Holy Spirit we may be truly wise and ever enjoy His consolations, Through Christ Our Lord, Amen. Jesus, I trust in You.

Laying Down Your Life

Sixth Sunday of Easter (Year B)

> "No one has greater love than this, to lay down one's life for one's friends." John 15:13

Love is very often understood as a strong feeling or emotion toward another. When someone is strongly attracted to someone or something, they "love it." But is this love? Is this love in the truest sense? Not really. Love certainly will have an emotional element to it but it will not be based on emotions or feelings.

So what is love? Love is a choice. Specifically, as Jesus identifies in the Gospel passage above, love is a choice to "lay down one's life for one's friends."

Laying down our lives indicates a number of things. First, it shows that the nature of love is a total self gift. Laying down your life cannot be done half way. Either your life is laid down or not. This reveals that love, in order for it to be love in the truest sense, is a total commitment of 100% of your life.

This passage also reveals that love is sacrificial. Laying down your life clearly shows that love requires a sort of death to self. It requires we look to the other first, putting their needs before ours. This requires true sacrifice and selflessness.

We lay down our lives for others in many ways. Some small, some big. Most importantly, we must foster an attitude of deep concern for the good of every person. When we do turn our eyes and hearts toward others, we will begin to discover countless ways to lay our lives down for them. Small acts of kindness, words of affirmation, a listening ear, help with a chore, etc. are a few of the small ways we give of ourselves every day. Greater acts may include a heroic forgiveness, love when we do not feel like being loving, giving mercy when it appears undeserved, and going out of our way to be there for a person when we do not have time in our busy schedule.

The bottom line is that giving of ourselves until it hurts turns any small or large sacrifice we give into a blessing for them and a glorious reward for us. Living a sacrificial life is fulfilling on many levels and is ultimately what we are made for.

Reflect, today, upon how well you lay down your life for others, holding nothing back. Do not hesitate to commit yourself to this depth of love. By giving yourself completely away you find yourself and discover the presence of our Divine Lord.

My sacrificial Lord, help me to put others first. Help me to love until it hurts. And in that loving sacrifice, help me to discover the love in Your own divine heart. Jesus, I trust in You.

The Love of God

Sixth Sunday of Easter (Year C)

> Jesus said to his disciples: "Whoever loves me will keep my word, and my Father will love him, and we will come to him and make our dwelling with him." John 14:23

Do you want our Lord to come to you and dwell within the depths of your soul? Presumably the answer is an easy "Yes." The way to make this happen is to love God and keep His word. When you do that, the Blessed Trinity will come and dwell within you.

It's interesting that the love of God appears to be contingent upon our love of Him. In other words, does God only love us when we love Him first? Strictly speaking, God loves us with a perfect love regardless of whether we love Him or not. But with that said, love takes on a whole new form when it is received and reciprocated. Therefore, when we choose to love God we suddenly realize that our love of Him opens the door for Him to come and dwell within us, transforming us and making our heart His holy sanctuary. What a glorious gift!

It's also interesting to note that love of God means, in part, that we are obedient to Him. But that's the nature of God. He is Love itself and, therefore, loving Him necessarily involves a complete submission of your will to His. Perfect obedience to Him in all things is a powerful way of loving Him. It's a way of allowing Him to dwell within you and, in that act, to take over your will. Only then can you love Him even more fully with your whole being.

Reflect, today, especially upon your desire to have the Most Holy Trinity come and dwell within your soul. This should be the primary goal of our lives. If God lives within us then all else in life will fall into place. All things will work for the good and God will be glorified in and through us. Make the choice to love Him through your obedience, this day, and your relationship of love will grow by leaps and bounds.

Most Holy Trinity, I do love You and desire to love You in a more perfect way this day. Help me to submit to Your perfect will in all things. Help me to embrace perfect obedience to You always. In that act of love and submission, come and make Your dwelling within me. Jesus, I trust in You.

Jesus Prepares Us

Monday of the Sixth Week of Easter

> "They will expel you from the synagogues; in fact, the hour is coming when everyone who kills you will think he is offering worship to God. They will do this because they have not known either the Father or me. I have told you this so that when their hour comes you may remember that I told you." John 16:2–4

Most likely, as the disciples listened to Jesus tell them they would be expelled from the synagogues and even killed, it went in one ear and out the other. Sure, it may have disturbed them a bit, but they most likely moved on rather quickly not worrying too much about it. But this is why Jesus said, "I have told you this so that when their hour comes you may remember that I told you." And you can be certain that when the disciples were persecuted by the scribes and Pharisees, they did remember these words of Jesus.

It must have been a heavy cross for them to receive such persecution from their religious leaders. Here, the people who were supposed to point them to God, were wreaking havoc in their lives. They would have been tempted to despair and lose their faith. But Jesus anticipated this heavy trial and, for that reason, warned them that it would come.

But what's interesting is what Jesus did not say. He did not tell them they should fight back, start a riot, form a revolution, etc. Rather, if you read the context to this statement, we see Jesus telling them that the Holy Spirit will take care of all things, will lead them and will enable them to testify to Jesus. To testify to Jesus is to be His witness. And to be a witness to Jesus is to be a martyr. Thus, Jesus prepared His disciples for their heavy cross of persecution by the religious leaders by letting them know that they would be strengthened by the Holy Spirit to give witness and testimony to Him. And once this began to take place, the disciples began to recall all that Jesus had told them.

You, too, must realize that being a Christian means persecution. We see this persecution in our world today through various terrorist attacks upon Christians. Some see it also, at times, within the "Domestic Church," the family, when they experience ridicule and harsh treatment for trying to live out their faith. And, sadly, it's even found within the Church itself when we see fighting, anger, disagreement and judgment.

The key is the Holy Spirit. The Holy Spirit plays a significant role right now in our world. That role is to strengthen us in our witness to Christ and to ignore any way the evil one would attack. So if you feel the pressure of persecution in any way, realize that Jesus spoke these words not only for His first disciples, but also for you.

Reflect, today, upon any way that you experience persecution in your life. Allow it to become an opportunity for hope and trust in the Lord through the outpouring of the Holy Spirit. He will never leave your side if you trust in Him.

Lord, when I feel the weight of the world or persecution, give me peace of mind and heart. Help strengthen me by the Holy Spirit that I may give joyful witness to You. Jesus, I trust in You.

Come Holy Spirit!

Tuesday of the Sixth Week of Easter

> "But I tell you the truth, it is better for you that I go. For if I do not go, the Advocate will not come to you. But if I go, I will send him to you." John 16:7

The hearts of the Apostles were conflicted. They were filled with grief, but they were also trying to trust what Jesus said to them. Jesus told them He was ascending to His Father and that it was better for them that He go. Why? Because if He goes, He will send the Holy Spirit to them.

On a human level, it would have been quite hard for the Apostles to let go of their daily interactions with Jesus. They certainly missed seeing Him with their eyes, touching Him and hearing Him. But Jesus made it clear that even though He was leaving He would be with them always. And He would also send the Holy Spirit upon them to lead them, give them courage, and teach them all truth. They would now be His presence in the world by the power of the Holy Spirit.

We never had the privilege of seeing Jesus in the way the Apostles did. But we do have the same privilege of Him being with us always. And we have the same privilege of receiving the fullness of the Holy Spirit. This is good. It is very good. But it is a good that we often miss. We may have been confirmed, but we may also still fail to let the Holy Spirit in and transform our lives.

In less than two weeks, we will celebrate the Solemnity of Pentecost. This is the annual celebration of the fulfillment of this promise of Jesus. On that day we commemorate the fact that the Holy Spirit has come and that we are now in the time of the Holy Spirit.

Reflect, today, and over the next couple of weeks about the Holy Spirit. Humbly admit to yourself if you need to let the

Holy Spirit become more alive in your life. Trust that Jesus wants you to receive Him in His fullness. And be not afraid to let this union take place.

Holy Spirit, please come to me. Help me to fan into flame Your presence in my life. May I receive You who was promised by Jesus in Your fullness. Holy Spirit, Divine Jesus, Merciful Father, I trust in You.

The Spirit of Truth

Wednesday of the Sixth Week of Easter

> Jesus said to his disciples: "I have much more to tell you, but you cannot bear it now. But when he comes, the Spirit of truth, he will guide you to all truth." John 16:12–13

As we continue to get closer to the wonderful Solemnity of Pentecost, we continue to focus in on the Holy Spirit. This passage specifically points to the Holy Spirit as the "Spirit of Truth."

It's interesting how Jesus introduces the Holy Spirit under this title. He explains that He has much more to tell them, but they cannot bear it now. In other words, the "Truth" is too much for them to bear unless the Holy Spirit is alive within them and teaching them. This gives us two wonderful insights worth pondering.

First, if we have not truly opened our lives to the power and presence of the Holy Spirit, we can be certain that we cannot bear the Truth. We cannot understand the deep truths of God and we cannot believe them unless the Holy Spirit is alive within us. That's a frightening thought in that, when the Holy Spirit is not fully immersing someone, that person is left in the dark regarding all Truth. And, sadly, they will not even realize they are in the dark!

If that does not make sense then perhaps you, too, suffer a bit from a lacking of the Spirit of Truth. Why? Because when the Spirit of Truth is alive within, you will know that you know the Truth.

Secondly, when you have fully opened your mind and heart to the Holy Spirit, you will become hungry for the Truth. The Holy Spirit will "guide you to all truth." And one of the effects of being guided into all truth is that you will be amazed with the journey. You will be in awe at the understanding of things that open up in your mind. You will be able to make sense of things in a new way. The Holy Spirit is the perfect "guide" and the journey toward the Truth is glorious.

Reflect, today, upon the Truth as it resides in the mind of the Father in Heaven. How open are you to the Truth? How fully do you embrace all that God wants to reveal to you? Open yourself more fully to the Holy Spirit and seek all that He wishes to reveal to you.

Holy Spirit, come consume my life. Teach me and guide me into all Truth. Holy Spirit, Divine Lord, Merciful Father, I trust in You.

Sorrow to Joy

Thursday of the Sixth Week of Easter (When the Ascension is transferred to Sunday)

> "Amen, amen, I say to you, you will weep and mourn, while the world rejoices; you will grieve, but your grief will become joy." John 16:20

Grief, mourning and even weeping is a part of life. Children will often weep at the slightest difficulty, but all of us face grief and sorrow throughout life.

In this passage above, Jesus informs His Apostles that sorrow and grief will be a part of their lives. This is a very sober but realistic statement on the part of our Lord. It's an act of love, on His part, to be up front with His Apostles about the coming hardships they will face.

The good news is that Jesus follows this statement with the hopeful news that their "grief will become joy." This is the most important part of what Jesus says.

The same is true in our lives. Jesus does not promise us that our lives will be free from hardship and pain. He does not tell us that following Him means that all will be easy in life. Instead, He wants us to know that we will follow in His footsteps if we choose to follow Him. He suffered, was mistreated and ultimately killed. And this would be tragic if He did not ultimately rise from the dead, ascend into Heaven and transform all prior grief and pain into the very means of the salvation of the world.

If we follow in His footsteps, we need to see every bit of grief in our lives as potentially a means of grace for many. If we can face the hardships of life with faith and hope, nothing will ultimately keep us down and everything will be able to be used for God's glory and will result in great joy.

Reflect, today, upon these words of Jesus. Know that He was not only speaking them to His Apostles, but also to you. Do not be scandalized or shocked when life deals you some difficulty. Do not despair when suffering is placed before you. Surrender all things to our Lord and let Him transform it into the joy that He promises in the end.

Lord of all hopefulness, I surrender to You all suffering in my life. My grief, hardships, sorrow and confusion I place in Your hands. I trust that You are all-powerful and desire to transform all things into a means of Your glory. Give me hope in times of despair and trust when life is hard. Jesus, I trust in You.

(In many dioceses throughout the world, the Feast of the Ascension is transferred to this coming Sunday)

The Continuing Presence of Our Lord

Solemnity of the Ascension of the Lord

So then the Lord Jesus, after he spoke to them, was taken up into heaven and took his seat at the right hand of God. But they went forth and preached everywhere, while the Lord worked with them and confirmed the word through accompanying signs. Mark 16:19–20 (Gospel from Year B)

Jesus completes His mission on Earth and ascends into Heaven to take His seat on His glorious throne for all eternity. Or does He? The answer is yes and no. Yes, He does take His seat on His glorious throne, but no, He does not complete His mission on Earth. The Ascension is both the end and the beginning. It's a transition to the next phase in the perfect plan of the Father. And understanding the way this plan unfolds should leave us in wonder and awe.

Sure, the Apostles were probably somewhat frightened and confused. Jesus was with them, then He died, then He rose and appeared various times, and then He ascended to the Father before their eyes. But He also told them that it is good that He goes. In fact, He said that it's better that He goes. They must have been confused. Jesus also told them His Advocate would come to lead them into all Truth. So the Apostles went from joy, to fear, to relief and more joy, to confusion and sorrow, to curiosity and uncertainty.

Sound familiar? Perhaps that's the way some find their lives to be. Ups and downs, twists and turns, joys and sorrows. Each phase reveals something new, something challenging, something glorious or something sorrowful. The good news is that the Father's plan is unfolding perfectly.

The part of the perfect plan we find ourselves in with this solemnity is the part where Jesus begins to direct His mission of establishing the Kingdom of God from Heaven. His throne is, in a sense, the driver's seat of our lives. From Heaven, Jesus suddenly begins to descend continuously into our lives fulfilling His mission in and through the Apostles, as well as all of us. The Ascension does not mean Jesus is gone; rather, it means Jesus is now present to each and every person who turns to Him and surrenders their life to His mission. From Heaven, Jesus is able to be present to all. He is able to live in us and invites us to live in Him. It's the new beginning of the Church. Now all the Apostles need to do is wait for the Holy Spirit to descend.

Reflect, today, upon the abiding and intimate presence of our Lord in your life. Know that Jesus invites you to share in His mission. From His glorious throne He wants us to "preach everywhere." He wants to invite each one of us to do our part. The part of the Father's plan entrusted to each one of us is not entrusted to another. We all have a share in that plan. What is your part? How does Jesus direct His mission through you? Ponder this question today and know that He accompanies you as you say "Yes" to your part in the glorious unfolding of His perfect plan.

My ascended Lord, I do find that my life is filled with many ups, downs, twists and turns. There are joys and sorrows, moments of confusion and clarity. In all things, help me to continually say "Yes" to Your plan. Jesus, I trust in You.

Anguish Turns to Joy

Friday of the Sixth Week of Easter

"When a woman is in labor, she is in anguish because her hour has arrived; but when she has given birth to a child, she no longer remembers the pain because of her joy that a child has been born into the world. So you also are now in anguish. But I will see you again,

Sixth Week of Easter

and your hearts will rejoice, and no one will take your joy away from you." John 16:21–22

Anguish in life is common. In small ways, we will experience anguish each and every day. And, from time to time, we will experience the very heavy pains of a particular anguish in our lives.

Does an experience of anguish mean you are not in God's grace? Does it mean that God has left you? Or does it mean that you are doing something wrong? Certainly not. In fact, all we have to do is look at the life of Jesus to see this is not the case. He was in constant anguish throughout His earthly life as He continually entered more deeply into the mission of His Father. Just prior to His public ministry He was in anguish for forty days in the desert. Throughout His public ministry, He experienced the anguish and exhaustion of His earthly life. He experienced the criticism of others, misunderstanding, ridicule, rejection, harsh treatment, and so much more. In the end, we know His fate on the Cross.

Our Blessed Mother had the "sword of sorrow" pierce her heart. She was misunderstood and ridiculed from the beginning as a result of her mysterious pregnancy out of wedlock. She carried a perfect love of her Son and anguished over His future as He grew. She watched many love Him and others harass Him. She watched His mockery of a trial and His Crucifixion.

But think of their lives now. They now reign from Heaven as the glorious Queen of All Saints and the King of the Universe. They live in glory now for eternity. Their anguish has turned to perfect joy.

Reflect, today, upon your own trials in life. The Scripture passage above reveals the promise that God makes to those who endure them with faith. If you feel as though you have been dealt an unfair hand or have been treated unfairly, you are in good company. The key is to walk through this life with grace and dignity. Do not let the trials of this life or its pains get you down. Know that as you remain faithful walking down the path God has set for you, the end result is that you will rejoice! This is simply a fact. Hold on to that hope and keep your eyes on the finish line. It's worth it in the end.

My compassionate Lord, I surrender my anguish and burdens to You. I unite them to Your Cross and trust that You will be there in all things walking with me through my life. May I keep my eyes on the goal and rejoice in Your steadfast love. Jesus, I trust in You.

Speaking Clearly

Saturday of the Sixth Week of Easter

"I have told you this in figures of speech. The hour is coming when I will no longer speak to you in figures but I will tell you clearly about the Father." John 16:25

Why does Jesus speak in "figures of speech" rather than speaking clearly? Good question.

We see this same fact in the many parables that Jesus spoke. Most likely, when people would hear His parables they would walk away asking, "What do you think He meant by that?" So why does Jesus speak in a veiled language rather than speaking clearly and directly?

The answer has to do with us and our lack of openness to the Truth. If we were fully open to the Truth, and if we were completely ready to embrace the Truth no matter what it was, Jesus would be able to speak to us clearly and we would respond immediately. But this is so rarely the way it happens. The key to understanding this is to understand the connection between knowledge of God's will and the willingness to immediately fulfill that will.

So often, we want Jesus to tell us His will, mull over it, consider it, and then come back with our response. But it doesn't happen that way. Rather, if we want Jesus to speak to us clearly, we must say yes to Him even before we know what He wants. Willingness to embrace His will is a prerequisite to understanding His will.

Of course our Blessed Mother is the perfect example of this in her fiat. Prior to the angel coming to her, she continually said "Yes" to the will of God. Then, when the angel came to her and told her what would happen, she asked for clarity. And she did indeed get that clarity as a direct response to her question. "The Holy Spirit will overshadow you and the power of the Most High will come upon you…" the angel said. But the only reason the angel, as a messenger of God, spoke so clearly was because she had already shown her heart to be fully compliant with God's plan no matter what it would be.

Reflect, today, upon how clearly you hear God speak to you. Do you want Him to be clearer to you? Do you want Him to speak to you with greater clarity? If so, work on surrendering your will over more completely to that which you do not even know. Say "Yes" to that which God wants of you tomorrow, and say "Yes" to it today. Building this habit of saying yes immediately will open the door to greater clarity in all God wants to say.

Lord, the answer is "Yes." I choose Your will today, tomorrow and always. I choose nothing but Your will. As I say "Yes" to You, help me to grow in greater clarity of all You ask of me. Jesus, I trust in You.

Seventh Week of Easter

(In many dioceses, the Solemnity of the Ascension is celebrated today. If you celebrate the Ascension in your diocese today, see the reflection from the previous Thursday)

The Prayer of Jesus

Seventh Sunday of Easter (When the Ascension was celebrated Thursday)

"Father, the hour has come. Give glory to your son, so that your son may glorify you, just as you gave him authority over all people, so that he may give eternal life to all you gave him." John 17:1–2 (Gospel from Year A)

John's Gospel, Chapter 17, is referred to as Jesus' High Priestly prayer. It's a long and beautiful prayer that would be worth reading in its entirety for reflection.

Jesus begins by speaking to the Father that "the hour has come." His hour of suffering and death is upon Him. But He sees it as an opportunity for His glorification. This is an important revelation within John's Gospel and especially within this prayer. The Cross is horrible from a human perspective alone. But from the divine perspective or the will of the Father and the salvation of the world, it is glorious and the moment in which Jesus takes up His throne of the Cross. It is glorious because He perfectly fulfills the will of the Father through His freely embraced suffering.

From there, Jesus prays for the Apostles in particular. He prays for their mission so that they will have the grace they need to also embrace the will of the Father and continue the work of Jesus. He knows that it is only by embracing their crosses, in accord with the will of the Father, that they will be able to be glorified.

Lastly, Jesus prays for those who would come to faith through the ministry of the Apostles. In particular, He prays for their unity. The unity Jesus is speaking of is a oneness that comes as a result of being united with the Father in Heaven. It is this oneness that leads to glorification for all. And, once again, this oneness is achieved only by being in full union with the will of the Father.

Reflect, today, upon this beautiful prayer and as you do, allow the Lord to speak to you. Hear Him calling you to perfect fulfillment and glory. But know that this is achieved by the embrace of your "hour." The Father is calling you to follow in the footsteps of His Son by laying down your life in perfect obedience to the Father's will. Embracing this cross is the path to Heaven and Jesus' prayer provides all the grace you need to say "Yes."

Father in Heaven, I choose to embrace Your perfect and holy will in all things. I accept from You the invitation to embrace my crosses in life and to enter into the hour to which You have called me. May I find true glory in this hour and may my life always give glory to You. Jesus, I trust in You.

Being Resolved

Monday of the Seventh Week of Easter

> "Now we realize that you know everything and that you do not need to have anyone question you. Because of this we believe that you came from God." Jesus answered them, "Do you believe now? Behold, the hour is coming and has arrived when each of you will be scattered to his own home and you will leave me alone." John 16:30–32

Have you come to believe in Jesus? How deep is that faith? And why do you believe? Are you ready and willing to hold on to that faith no matter what comes your way? Are you ready to follow Him even if it's difficult and unpopular? Are you ready to suffer as a result of your faith? These are

Seventh Week of Easter

important questions. They are questions that we must answer both when it's easy to be a Christian as well as when it's hard.

It's easy to be a Christian and to follow Jesus when everyone else is doing it. For example, at a baptism or wedding it's normal to want to belong and to let others know of our support and belief in what they are doing. But what about those moments when your faith is ridiculed or put down? Or when you have to make the difficult choice to turn from cultural pressures and stand out for your faith? These are more challenging times to be a follower of Christ.

In today's Gospel, there were many who had been analyzing Jesus' teaching, listening to Him and talking about Him. It seems clear that the consensus was that Jesus was a man of holiness and a great prophet. Many were even coming to believe He was the Messiah. So there was a sort of positive momentum present that made it easier for many people to say that they believed in Him and they believed that He came from God.

Jesus quickly points out to them that, though they believe now, there will be a time that comes soon when most everyone will abandon Him, when they are scattered, and they will leave Him alone. This is obviously a prophecy of His coming persecution and Crucifixion.

One of the greatest tests of our faith is to look at how faithful we are when following Christ is not all that popular. It is in these moments, more than the easy moments, that we have an opportunity to manifest our faith and deepen our resolve to be a Christian.

Reflect, today, on how deep your commitment to Christ goes. Are you ready to follow Him to the Cross? Are you willing to give up everything to Follow Him? Hopefully the answer is a definitive yes. It must be a "Yes" that directs our lives no matter the situation of life we find ourselves in.

Lord, I do believe. Help me to let that faith in You stay strong at all times. Help me to say yes to You and to live that yes always. Jesus, I trust in You.

Glorification

Tuesday of the Seventh Week of Easter

> Jesus raised his eyes to heaven and said, "Father, the hour has come. Give glory to your son, so that your son may glorify you." John 17:1

Giving glory to the Son is an act of the Father, but is also an act to which we should all be attentive!

First of all, we should recognize the "hour" that Jesus speaks of as the hour of His Crucifixion. This may, at first, seem like a sad moment. But, from a divine perspective, Jesus sees it as His hour of glory. It's the hour when He is glorified by the Father in Heaven because He perfectly fulfilled the Father's will. He perfectly embraced His death for the salvation of the world.

We must also see this from our human perspective. From the standpoint of our daily lives, we must see that this "hour" is something that we can continually embrace and bring to fruition. The "hour" of Jesus is something that we must constantly live. How? By constantly embracing the Cross in our lives so that this cross is also a moment of glorification. In doing this, our crosses take on a divine perspective, becoming divinized so as to become a source of the grace of God.

The beauty of the Gospel is that every suffering we endure, every cross we carry, is an opportunity to manifest the Cross of Christ. We are called, by Him, to constantly give Him glory by living His suffering and death in our lives.

Reflect, today, upon the hardships you endure. And know that, in Christ, those hardships can share in His redeeming love if you let Him.

Jesus, I surrender my cross and my hardships over to You. You are God and You are able to transform all things into glory. Jesus, I trust in You.

Surviving This World

Wednesday of the Seventh Week of Easter

> "I gave them your word, and the world hated them, because they do not belong to the world any more than I belong to the world. I do not ask that you take them out of the world but that you keep them from the Evil One. They do not belong to the world any more than I belong to the world. Consecrate them in the truth. Your word is truth." John 17:14–17

"Consecrate them in the truth. Your word is truth." That's the key to survival!

Scripture reveals three primary temptations we face in life: The flesh, the world and the devil. All three of these work to lead us astray. But all three are conquerable with one thing...the Truth.

This Gospel passage above specifically speaks of the "world" and the "evil one." The evil one, who is the devil, is real. He hates us and does all he can to mislead us and ruin our lives. He tries to fill our minds with empty promises, offers fleeting pleasure, and encourages selfish ambitions. He was a liar from the beginning and remains a liar to this day.

One of the temptations that the devil threw at Jesus during His forty day fast at the beginning of His public ministry was a temptation to obtain all the world has to offer. The devil showed Jesus all the kingdoms of the Earth and said, "All these I shall give to you, if you will prostrate yourself and worship me."

First of all, this was a silly temptation given the fact that Jesus already was the Creator of all things. But, nonetheless, He allowed the devil to tempt Him with this worldly enticement. Why did He do this? Because Jesus knew we would all be tempted with the many enticements of the world. By "world" we mean many things. One thing that comes to mind, in our day and age, is the desire for worldly acceptance. This is a plague that is very subtle but affects so many, including our Church itself.

With the powerful influence of the media and the global political culture, there is pressure today, more than ever, for us as Christians to simply conform to our age. We are tempted to do and believe what is popular and socially acceptable. And the "gospel" we are allowing ourselves to hear is the secular world of moral indifferentism.

There is a powerful cultural tendency (a global tendency due to the Internet and media) to become people who are willing to accept anything and everything. We have lost our sense of moral integrity and truth. Thus, the words of Jesus need to be embraced more today than ever. "Your Word is Truth." The Word of God, the Gospel, all that our Catechism teaches, all that our faith reveals is the Truth. This Truth must be our guiding light and nothing else.

Reflect, today, on how much of an influence the secular culture has on you. Have you given into secular pressure, or the secular "gospels" of our day and age? It takes a strong person to resist these lies. We will resist them only if we stay consecrated in the Truth.

Lord of all Truth, I do consecrate myself to You. You are the Truth. Your Word is what I need to stay focused and to navigate through the many lies all around me. Give me strength and wisdom so that I may always remain in Your protection away from the evil one. Jesus, I trust in You.

Lifting Your Eyes to Heaven

Thursday of the Seventh Week of Easter

> Lifting up his eyes to heaven, Jesus prayed saying: "I pray not only for these, but also for those who will believe in me through their word, so that they may all be one, as you, Father, are in me and I in you, that they also may be in us, that the world may believe that you sent me." John 17:20–21

"Lifting His eyes to Heaven…" What a great phrase!

As Jesus lifted His eyes to Heaven, He prayed to His Father in Heaven. This act, of lifting His eyes, reveals one unique aspect of the presence of the Father. It reveals that the Father is transcendent. "Transcendent" means that the Father is above all and beyond all. The world cannot contain Him. So, in speaking to the Father, Jesus begins with this gesture by which He acknowledges the transcendence of the Father.

But we must also note the imminence of the Father's relationship with Jesus. By "imminence" we mean that the Father and Jesus are united as one. Their relationship is one that is profoundly personal in nature.

Though these two words, "imminence" and "transcendence," may not be a part of our daily vocabulary, the concepts are worth understanding and reflecting upon. We should strive to be very familiar with their meanings and, more specifically, with the way that our relationship with the Holy Trinity shares in both.

Jesus' prayer to the Father was that we who come to believe will share in the unity of the Father and the Son. We will share in God's life and love. For us, this means we start by seeing the transcendence of God. We also lift our eyes to Heaven and strive to see the splendor, glory, greatness, power, and majesty of God. He is above all and beyond all.

As we accomplish this prayerful gaze to the Heavens, we must also strive to see this glorious and transcendent God descend into our souls, communicating to us, loving us, and establishing a deeply personal relationship with us. It's amazing how these two aspects of God's life go together so well even though, at first, they can appear to be complete opposites. They are not opposed but, rather, are wedded together and have the effect of drawing us into an intimate relationship with the Creator and sustainer of all things.

Reflect, today, upon the glorious and all-powerful God of the Universe descending into the secret depths of your soul. Acknowledge His presence, adore Him as He lives within you, speak to Him and love Him.

Most glorious Lord, help me to always lift my eyes to Heaven in prayer. May I constantly turn to You and Your Father. In that prayerful gaze, may I also discover You alive in my soul where You are adored and loved. Jesus, I trust in You.

Do You Love Me?

Friday of the Seventh Week of Easter

> He said to him the third time, "Simon, son of John, do you love me?" Peter was distressed that he had said to him a third time, "Do you love me?" and he said to him, "Lord, you know everything; you know that I love you." Jesus said to him, "Feed my sheep." John 21:17

Three times Jesus asked Peter if he loved Him. Why three times? One reason was so that Peter could "make up" for the three times he denied Jesus. No, Jesus did not need Peter to apologize three times, but Peter needed to express his love three times and Jesus knew it.

Three is also a number of perfection. For example, we say God is "Holy, Holy, Holy." This triple expression is a way of saying that God is the Holiest of all. By Peter being given the opportunity to tell Jesus three times that He loved Him it was an opportunity for Peter to express His love in the deepest of ways.

So we have a triple confession of love and a triple undoing of Peter's denial going on. This should reveal to us our own need to love God and seek His mercy in a "triple" way.

When you tell God that you love Him, how deep does that go? Is it more a service of words, or is it a total and all-consuming love? Is your love of God something that you mean to the fullest extent? Or is it something that needs work?

Certainly we all need to work on our love, and that is why this passage should be so significant to us. We should hear Jesus asking us this question three times also. We should realize that He is not satisfied with a simple, "Lord, I love You." He wants to hear it again, and again. He asks us this because He knows we need to express this love in the deepest way. "Lord, You know everything, You know that I love You!" This must be our ultimate answer.

This triple question also gives us the opportunity to express our deepest longing for His mercy. We all sin. We all deny Jesus in one way or another. But the good news is that Jesus is always inviting us to let our sin be a motivation for deepening our love. He doesn't sit and stay angry at us. He doesn't pout. He doesn't hold our sin over our heads. But He does ask for the deepest of sorrow and a complete conversion of heart. He wants us to turn from our sin to the fullest extent.

Reflect, today, upon the depth of your love for God and how well you express it to Him. Make a choice to express your love for God in a triple way. Let it be deep, sincere and irrevocable. The Lord will receive this heartfelt act and return it to you a hundredfold.

My loving Lord, You do know that I love You. You also know how weak I am. Let me hear Your invitation to express my love for You and my desire for Your mercy. May I offer this love and desire to the fullest extent. Jesus, I trust in You.

Jesus' Hidden Life
Saturday of the Seventh Week of Easter

There are also many other things that Jesus did, but if these were to be described individually, I do not think the whole world would contain the books that would be written. John 21:25

Imagine the insights that our Blessed Mother would have had about her Son. She, as His mother, would have seen and understood so many hidden moments of His life. She would have watched Him grow year after year. She would have watched Him relate and interact with others throughout His life. She would have noticed that He was preparing for His public ministry. And she would have witnessed so many hidden moments of that public ministry and countless sacred moments of His entire life.

This Scripture above is the final sentence of the Gospel of John and is one we do not hear very often. But it offers some fascinating insights to reflect upon. All we know about the life of Christ is contained in the Gospels, but how could these short Gospel books ever come close to describing the totality of who Jesus is? They certainly cannot. To do that, as John says above, the pages could not be contained in the whole world. That's saying a lot.

So a first insight we should take from this Scripture is that we know only a small portion of the actual life of Christ. What we know is glorious. But we should realize that there is so much more. And this realization should fill our minds with interest, longing and a desire for more. By coming to know how little we actually do know, we will hopefully be compelled to seek Christ more deeply.

However, a second insight we can gain from this passage is that, even though the numerous events of Christ's life cannot be contained in countless volumes of books, we can, nonetheless, discover Jesus Himself in what IS contained in the Holy Scriptures. No, we may not know every detail of His life, but we can come to meet the Person. We can come to encounter the Living Word of God Himself in the Scriptures and, in that encounter and meeting of Him, we are given all we need.

Reflect, today, on how deeply you know Jesus. Do you spend sufficient time reading the Scriptures and meditating on them? Do you speak to Him daily and seek to know and love Him? Is He present to you and do you regularly make yourself present to Him? If the answer to any of these questions is "No" then perhaps this is a good day to recommit yourself to a deeper reading of the Sacred Word of God.

Lord, I may not know everything about Your life, but I do desire to know You. I desire to meet You every day, to love You and to know You. Help me to enter more deeply into a relationship with You. Jesus, I trust in You.

Feasts and Solemnities

The Infallible Gift from Jesus

Feast of the Chair of St. Peter, February 22

> "And so I say to you, you are Peter, and upon this rock I will build my Church, and the gates of the netherworld shall not prevail against it. I will give you the keys to the Kingdom of heaven. Whatever you bind on earth shall be bound in heaven; and whatever you loose on earth shall be loosed in heaven." Matthew 16:18–19

This passage should give us great comfort. Why? Because in this passage Jesus lays the foundation of His Church. He gives to Peter the keys to the Kingdom of Heaven. And, in so doing, He establishes what has come to be known as the gift of "infallibility."

Think about it. What does it mean to be given "the keys to the Kingdom of Heaven?" This is quite a statement. But by speaking it clearly and definitively, Jesus entrusted an incredible spiritual power to Peter. He may not have understood what this exactly meant at the time, but he would have been changed as he was entrusted with such authority.

By "infallibility" we mean that Peter was guaranteed to teach only that which was true in the areas of faith and morality. Faith and morality are what live on forever in the Kingdom of Heaven and so it is with authority in these areas that Peter is entrusted.

Furthermore, we know that the Apostles had successors. Peter went to Rome and became the Bishop of Rome. He was succeeded by Linus, then Cletus, then Clement, and so forth until the Bishop of Rome today. In 2013, Pope Francis became the 265th successor of St. Peter. This is important to note because this spiritual authority that Jesus gave to Peter did not end with his death. Rather, it continued with his successors and will continue on until the end of the world.

Today, in celebrating the great Feast of the Chair of St. Peter, we not only honor the Pope, we also rejoice in the spiritual authority that the Holy Father has been entrusted with. And knowing that Jesus is alive in such a way, through the certain teaching authority of the Keys of Heaven, we should be comforted and at peace knowing that the gates of hell will never prevail against the Church. Popes are sinners, but they are also visible and infallible instruments of Christ Himself every time they exercise their sacred role.

Reflect, today, upon your faith in the Church. We do not put our faith in persons, we put our faith in Christ, His Church and in the spiritual authority entrusted to the Church. Reflect upon your own faith in this regard and if it is lacking in any way, renew it in honor of this great Feast of the Chair of St. Peter.

Lord Jesus, You entrusted Your power and authority to St. Peter and to all of his successors. I thank You for the gift of our pope. I pray for him and offer him to You for Your guidance and protection. I renew my faith in the gift of the Holy Father and in Your promise to lead us always through him. May my faith in Your Church bring me consolation and hope as we all move forward to the goal of our salvation, the glorious Kingdom of Heaven. Jesus, I trust in You.

Solemnities and Feasts

Unwavering Faith in the Face of Confusion
Solemnity of Saint Joseph, Husband of Mary, March 19

> Joseph, son of David, do not be afraid to take Mary your wife into your home. For it is through the Holy Spirit that this child has been conceived in her. She will bear a son and you are to name him Jesus, because he will save his people from their sins. Matthew 1:20

What a blessed man St. Joseph was. He was called to be the earthly father of the Son of God and the husband of the Mother of God! He must have been in awe of this responsibility and he must have, at times, trembled with a holy fear in the face of so great a calling.

What's interesting to note, however, is that the beginning of this call seemed to be marked with an apparent scandal. Mary was pregnant and it was not from Joseph. How could this be? The only earthly explanation was infidelity on Mary's part. But this was so contrary to whom Joseph perceived her to be. He certainly would have been quite shocked and quite confused as he faced this apparent dilemma. What should he do?

We know what he decided to do at first. He decided to divorce her quietly. But then the angel spoke to him in a dream. And, after he awoke from his sleep, "he did as the angel of the Lord had commanded him and took his wife into his home."

One aspect of this situation to ponder is the fact that Joseph had to embrace his wife and her Son in faith. This new family of his was beyond human reason alone. There was no way to make sense of it simply by trying to figure it out. He had to approach it with faith.

Faith means he had to rely upon the voice of God speaking to him in his conscience. Yes, he relied on what the angel spoke to him in the dream, but that was a dream! People can have all sorts of strange dreams! His human tendency would be to question this dream and wonder if this was real. Was this really from God? Is this Child truly from the Holy Spirit? How could this be?

All of these questions, and every other question that would have arisen in St. Joseph's mind, could only be answered by faith. But the good news is that faith does give answers. Faith enables a person to face the confusions of life with strength, conviction and certitude. Faith opens up the door to peace in the midst of uncertainty. It eliminates fear and replaces it with the joy of knowing you are following God's will. Faith works and faith is what we all need in life to survive.

Reflect, today, upon the depth of your faith in the face of apparent difficulties. If you feel God calling you to enter into some challenge in your life right now, follow the example of St. Joseph. Let God say to you, "Do not be afraid!" He spoke this to St. Joseph and He speaks it to you. God's ways are far above our ways, His thoughts far above our thoughts, His wisdom far above our wisdom. God had a perfect plan for St. Joseph's life, and He does for you too. Walk by faith each and every day and you will see that glorious plan unfold.

Lord, enable me to walk by faith each and every day. Allow my mind to rise above human wisdom alone and to see Your divine plan in all things. St. Joseph, pray for me that I may imitate the faith you lived in your own life. St. Joseph, pray for us. Jesus, I trust in You!

God Becomes Man—Nine Months Before Christmas
Solemnity of the Annunciation, March 25

> Then the angel said to her, "Do not be afraid, Mary, for you have found favor with God. Behold, you will conceive in your womb and bear a son, and you shall name him Jesus. He will be great and will be called Son of the Most High, and the Lord God will give him the throne of David his father, and he will rule over the house of Jacob forever, and of his Kingdom there will be no end." Luke 1:30–33

Happy Solemnity! We celebrate today one of the most glorious feast days of the year. Today is nine months before Christmas and is the day we celebrate the fact that God the Son took on our human nature in the womb of the Blessed Virgin. It's the celebration of the Incarnation of our Lord.

There are many things to celebrate today and many things for which we should be eternally grateful. First and foremost we celebrate the profound fact that God loves us so much that He became one of us. The fact that God took on our human nature is worthy of unlimited rejoicing and celebration! If we only understood what this meant. If we could only understand the effects of this incredible event in history. The fact that God became a human being in the womb of the Blessed Virgin is a gift beyond our comprehension. It's a gift that elevates humanity to the realm of the divine. God and man are united in this glorious event and we should be forever grateful.

We also see in this event the glorious act of perfect submission to the will of God. We see this in the Blessed Mother herself. It's interesting to note that our Blessed Mother was told that "you will conceive in your womb and bear a son..." She wasn't asked by the angel if she was willing, rather, she was told what was to happen. Why is that the case?

It happened this way because the Blessed Virgin said yes to God throughout her life. Never was there a moment that she said no to God. Therefore, her perpetual yes to God enabled the angel Gabriel to tell her that she "will conceive." In other words, the angel was able to tell her what she had already said yes to in her life.

What a glorious example this is. Our Blessed Mother's "Yes" is an incredible witness to us. We are called to daily say yes to God. And we are called to say yes to Him even before we know what He asks of us. This solemnity affords us the opportunity to once again say "Yes" to the will of God. No matter what He is asking of you, the right answer is "Yes."

Reflect, today, upon your own invitation from God to say "Yes" to Him in all things. You, like our Blessed Mother, are invited to bring our Lord into the world. Not in the literal way she did, but you are called to be an instrument of His continual Incarnation in our world. Reflect upon how fully you answer this call and get on your knees today and say "Yes" to the plan our Lord has for your life.

Lord, the answer is "Yes!" Yes, I choose your divine will. Yes, You may do with me whatever You will. May my "Yes" be as pure and holy as our Blessed Mother's. Let it be done to me according to Your will. Jesus, I trust in You.

Being an Evangelist

Feast of Saint Mark, April 25

> "These signs will accompany those who believe: in my name they will drive out demons, they will speak new languages. They will pick up serpents with their hands, and if they drink any deadly thing, it will not harm them. They will lay hands on the sick, and they will recover." Mark 16:17–18

Did Jesus mean this literally? Yes. He certainly did. And throughout the history of the Church we have seen great miracles and mighty deeds performed by His followers in His name as God willed it in various times and places. So, yes, He meant what He said.

But there is also another level of meaning we should not miss. Though this is not literally going to be lived out by everyone who believes, it will be lived out according to a deeper and spiritual meaning.

There are four basic things Jesus promises will happen here. He promises that those who have faith will: 1) be victorious over the evil one, 2) communicate in a new way, 3) face worldly dangers and be protected, and 4) be a source of healing for others.

First, the evil one is real and is constantly trying to frighten us and overwhelm us. But, by analogy, the evil one is like a 3-pound dog who has a vicious and obnoxious bark, and little bite. The "barking" may be frightening at times, but the power of Christ is like a steel-toed boot that can easily handle this menace.

Second, we are called to "speak new languages" in that we are called to communicate the words and truth of God in a way that is beyond our natural abilities. We are called to speak and communicate in the language of God and to become His mouth for a world in need.

Third, there will be many struggles we face in this life. Not only from the evil one, but also from the world and from our own distorted struggles. Again, Jesus promises the grace to overcome the many dangers and struggles we will face in life if we but let Him.

Lastly, Jesus came to heal, especially our souls, and he wants us to be instruments of healing for those whom we encounter every day.

St. Mark, whom we honor today, was a great evangelist for Christ. Reflect, today, upon the fact that we are all called to share in the mission of evangelization. Ponder these callings in life as outlined above and if one stands out and speaks to you in a unique way, listen to it carefully. It may be God calling you to share more fully in His divine mission.

Lord, I do believe and I do choose to let You use me as an instrument of Your grace. May the faith You have given me be also a source of grace for a world in need. Jesus, I trust in You.

Jesus Calls the Weak

Feast of Saints Philip and James, Apostles, May 3

> Philip said to Jesus, "Master, show us the Father, and that will be enough for us." Jesus said to him, "Have I been with you for so long a time and you still do not know me, Philip?" John 14:8–9

We honor two of the Apostles today, Philip and James the Lesser. We know very little about James other than that he was chosen by our Lord for the apostolic ministry. We also have one of his letters which is contained in the New Testament. After the Resurrection, Jesus appeared to James who eventually went to Jerusalem and led the Church for a few decades, eventually being stoned as a martyr.

Philip is known from some of his comments that appear to reveal a weakness of faith. In addition to the comment above, recall when Jesus was preparing to multiply the fish and loaves and asked Philip, "Where can we buy enough food for them to eat?" (John 6:5). Philip's response was, "Two hundred days' wages worth of food would not be enough for each of them to have a little bit" (John 6:7). But Jesus was testing Philip and, unfortunately, he failed the test.

But Philip did not continue to fail in his faith. Recall, also, that Philip is the one who was inspired to baptize the Ethiopian eunuch in the Acts of the Apostles. Eventually, tradition states that Philip preached in Greece, Phrygia, and Syria. He and Saint Bartholomew were said to have been crucified upside down. Tradition holds that Philip preached upside down from the cross until his death.

In the end, James and Philip gave their lives for Christ, holding nothing back. But it took time for them to grow in faith and confidence in Jesus. This is a significant witness for our lives.

Ideally, our response to Jesus every day will be that of a complete submission to Him and perfect trust in His divine will. Ideally, we will not lack faith.

However, it's most likely the case that all of us can look back at many moments in our lives and point to ways in which we have failed in our faith and trust in our Lord. Though this is sin, it's good to look at these moments of weakness in the light of the mercy of God. Jesus saw the weakness of Philip, addressed it, but continued to love him and continued to call him down the path chosen for him. Jesus does the same with each one of us.

Reflect, today, upon any ways that you can identify with the doubts and weaknesses of the Apostle Philip. See those weaknesses for what they are: your sin. But allow yourself to grow in hope today as we honor Philip and James. The Lord never gave up on them and He will not give up on you. He continued to call them to a holy and sacred ministry, and He will continue to do the same for you.

Lord, I thank You for never giving up on me, even when I sin and turn away from You. Help me to persevere in my faith in You and to answer the call to radically follow You wherever You lead. Sts. James and Philip, pray for us. Jesus, I trust in You.

The Apostolic Ministry
Feast of Saint Matthias, Apostle, May 14

> Peter said... "Therefore, it is necessary that one of the men who accompanied us the whole time the Lord Jesus came and went among us, beginning from the baptism of John until the day on which he was taken up from us, become with us a witness to his resurrection." So they proposed two, Joseph called Barsabbas, who was also known as Justus, and Matthias. Then they prayed, "You, Lord, who know the hearts of all, show which one of these two you have chosen to take the place in this apostolic ministry from which Judas turned away to go to his own place." Then they gave lots to them, and the lot fell upon Matthias, and he was counted with the Eleven Apostles. Acts 1:21–26

And with that we have the first new bishop!

The Feast of St. Matthias is a celebration of the continuation of the apostolic ministry. By honoring St. Matthias we honor the fact that Jesus enabled His first Apostles to pass on the sacred power of their ordination to others as their successors. St. Matthias took the place of Judas. And as the Church continued to grow, there were others picked and given the grace of ordination as bishops.

Solemnities and Feasts

Today, every one of our bishops has a direct line of succession to one or more of the Apostles. This unbroken succession is our direct connection to the priestly ministry of Jesus as it is passed on to the Church.

What a gift this is! It's true that not every bishop or priest is a saint. We are all quite aware of that. But it is also true that every bishop and priest shares in the wonderful gift of Christ's priestly ministry. And this ministry is not for them, it's for you.

Jesus desired that He continue His ministry in a concrete, personal and human way. He desired that He would be present at every Baptism, Confirmation and Holy Communion. He desired to personally be there administering these graces to His people. And He is there, through the ministry of the bishop or priest.

The key is to see Christ in that ministry. Every priest or bishop is a unique representation of Christ in his own way. They each reflect Christ in their human personality and holiness. But, more importantly, they represent Christ by acting in His very person. Jesus speaks His words of absolution and consecration through them. So we need to see beyond the surface and see Christ Jesus. This is entirely possible if we approach God's ministers in faith.

Reflect, today, upon the way you approach God's priests and bishops. How do you speak about them? Do you seek Christ in them? Are you open to Christ ministering through them? The apostolic ministry in which they share is a true gift from Christ and must be loved and accepted as if we were accepting Christ Himself...because that's exactly what we are doing.

Lord, thank You for the gift of your ordained ministers. Thank you for the bishop and for all the priests who have ministered Your Word and Sacraments to me. I pray for them today that they may continue to be holy instruments of Your love. Jesus, I trust in You.

Most Blessed Are You Among Women!

Feast of the Visitation of the Blessed Virgin Mary, May 31

> Elizabeth, filled with the Holy Spirit, cried out in a loud voice and said, "Blessed are you among women, and blessed is the fruit of your womb. And how does this happen to me, that the mother of my Lord should come to me?" Luke 1:41b–43

What an honor it would be to have our Blessed Mother, the mother of Jesus, come to us for a visit. Elizabeth was keenly aware of this honor and, as a result, she cried out in an inspired way acknowledging that fact.

Though this was a unique gift given to Elizabeth, to have the mother of her Lord come to her, we must understand that we are all equally blessed by the opportunity to daily invite the presence of the Mother of God into our lives.

Mother Mary is the Queen of all Saints, but she is also the Queen of all sinners and Queen of those striving for holiness. She is the Mother of All the Living and the Mother of the Church. In God's providence, she continues to carry out her unique role of visiting those in need on a daily basis. She does so in a way that is far more profound and transformative than in the case of Elizabeth. Mother Mary's visits to us, her children, now takes place in the order of grace.

What does it mean when we say that our Blessed Mother visits us in the order of grace? It means that our relationship with her is based on the divine will and plan of God. It means we are able to have a relationship with her by which she communicates to us countless mercies from her Son. It means that she becomes the most powerful mediatrix of grace for us that the world has ever known. It means that the effect she has in our lives is deep, profound, transformative and intimately personal.

The difficult part about a relationship with our Blessed Mother is that it must take place on a spiritual and interior level rather than on a physical and exterior one. However, even though this is the case, we should not think that this means we are less capable of knowing her and loving her. In fact, the relationship we are now able to have with our Blessed Mother by grace is far deeper and more profound than the relationship Elizabeth was able to have with her on account of the Visitation.

Reflect, today, upon your relationship with the Mother of God. She visited Elizabeth long ago and now desires to visit your soul so as to bring you the grace and mercy of her Son. Seek to establish this beautiful relationship with her in the order of grace. Invite her in, listen to her, be open to the grace she brings to you and rejoice with Elizabeth that the mother of your Lord would come to you.

Dearest Mother Mary, I love you and consecrate my life to You, trusting in your motherly care and mediation. Help me, dear Mother, to be open to all that you desire to bring to me from your Son, Jesus. I am honored and humbled that you would care for me and desire to bring to me the mercy of the Heart of your Son Jesus. Mother Mary, pray for us. Jesus, I trust in You.

The Coming of the Holy Spirit

Solemnity of Pentecost Sunday

And suddenly there came from the sky a noise like a strong driving wind, and it filled the entire house in which they were. Then there appeared to them tongues as of fire, which parted and came to rest on each one of them. And they were all filled with the Holy Spirit and began to speak in different tongues, as the Spirit enabled them to proclaim. Acts 2:2–4

Do you think there was really a "noise like a strong driving wind" at this first outpouring of the Holy Spirit? And do you think there really were "tongues as of fire" that came and rested on everyone? Well, there most likely was! Why else would it have been recorded that way in the Scriptures?

These physical manifestations of the coming of the Holy Spirit were made present for numerous reasons. One reason was so that these first recipients of the full outpouring of the Holy Spirit would have concretely understood that something amazing was happening. By seeing and hearing these physical manifestations of the Holy Spirit they were more properly disposed to understand that God was doing something awesome. And then, upon seeing and hearing these manifestations, they were touched by the Holy Spirit, consumed, filled and set on fire. They suddenly discovered within themselves the promise Jesus made and they finally began to understand. Pentecost changed their lives!

We most likely have not seen and heard these physical manifestations of the outpouring of the Holy Spirit, but we should rely upon the witness of those in the Scriptures to allow ourselves to arrive at a deep and transforming faith that the Holy Spirit is real and wants to enter our lives in the same way. God wants to set our hearts on fire with His love, strength and grace so as to effectively live lives that effect change in the world. Pentecost is not only about us becoming holy, it's also about us being given all we need to go forth and bring the holiness of God to all those we encounter. Pentecost enables us to be powerful instruments of the transforming grace of God. And there is no doubt that the world around us needs this grace.

As we celebrate Pentecost, it would be helpful to ponder the primary effects of the Holy Spirit in a prayerful way. Below are the Seven Gifts of the Holy Spirit. These Gifts are the primary effects of Pentecost for each and every one of us. Use them as an examination of your life and let God show you where you need to grow more deeply in the strength of the Holy Spirit.

Lord, send forth Your Spirit in my life and set me on fire with the Gifts of Your Spirit. Holy Spirit, I invite You to take possession of my soul. Come Holy Spirit, come and transform my life. Holy Spirit, I trust in You.

Seven Gifts of the Holy Spirit

Fear of the Lord: With this gift the Christian becomes keenly aware of anything that may hurt his/her relationship with God. There is a holy "fear" of hurting this relationship and grace is given to avoid these things at all cost.

Wisdom: With this gift the Christian is given a special grace to "ponder divine realities" in his/her speculative reason. We are able to see the big picture and know how best to be an instrument of peace and harmony in our world.

Understanding: This is the ability to have a supernatural assurance of the matters of faith. Life makes sense. We can make sense of the deeper parts of revelation, make sense of suffering and understand those things that tempt us to doubt. With this gift we come to see how everything in life can work for good in accordance with God's plan.

Knowledge: With this gift the Christian knows, more in the practical intellect, what God's will is in this or that situation. We know how to live, how to discern God's will and what decision to make in our daily life. It also enables us to learn from our past mistakes.

Counsel: With this gift the Christian sees him/herself as a link in a chain which makes up the entire Church. God uses each one of us to help and support one another on our journey. We know what to say and how to act so as to do our part to build up one another.

Fortitude: Simply put, it is a firmness of mind and spirit to do good and avoid evil. It's a sort of Christian courage. The Gospel will call all of us to a radical life of love. Fortitude gives us the strength we need to follow through.

Piety: This gift enables us to first reverence and love God, but also to see the dignity of one another and reverence each other as children of God.

The Cross, the Eucharist and the Blessed Mother

Memorial of the Blessed Virgin Mary, Mother of the Church—Monday after Pentecost

> When Jesus saw his mother and the disciple there whom he loved, he said to his mother, "Woman, behold, your son." Then he said to the disciple, "Behold, your mother." And from that hour the disciple took her into his home. John 19:26–27

On March 3, 2018, Pope Francis announced that a new memorial would be celebrated on the Monday after Pentecost Sunday, entitled "The Blessed Virgin Mary, Mother of the Church." Henceforth, this memorial is added to the General Roman Calendar and is to be universally celebrated throughout the Church.

In instituting this memorial, Cardinal Robert Sarah, Prefect of the Congregation for Divine Worship, said:

> This celebration will help us to remember that growth in the Christian life must be anchored to the Mystery of the Cross, to the oblation of Christ in the Eucharistic Banquet and to the Mother of the Redeemer and Mother of the Redeemed, the Virgin who makes her offering to God.

"Anchored" to the *Cross*, the *Eucharist*, and the *Blessed Virgin Mary* who is both "Mother of the Redeemer" and "Mother of the Redeemed." What beautiful insights and inspiring words from this holy Cardinal of the Church.

The Gospel chosen for this memorial presents to us the holy image of the Blessed Mother standing before the Cross of her Son. While standing there, she heard Jesus say the words, "I thirst." He was given some wine on a sponge and then declared, "It is finished." Jesus' Blessed Mother, the Mother of the Redeemer, stood as a witness as the Cross of her Son became the source of the redemption of the World. As He took that last drink of wine, He completed the institution of the New and Eternal Passover Meal, the Holy Eucharist.

Additionally, just prior to Jesus expiring, Jesus declared to His mother that she would now be the "Mother of the Redeemed," that is, the mother of each member of the Church. This gift of Jesus' mother to the Church was symbolized by Him saying, "Behold, your son...Behold, your mother."

As we celebrate this new and beautiful universal memorial within the Church, ponder your relationship to the Cross, to the Eucharist and to your heavenly mother. If you are willing to stand by the Cross, gaze at it with our Blessed Mother, and witness Jesus pour forth His precious blood for the salvation of the world, then you are also privileged to hear Him say to you, "Behold, your mother." Stay close to your heavenly mother. Seek her maternal care and protection and allow her prayers to daily draw you closer to her Son.

Dearest Mother Mary, Mother of God, my mother, and Mother of the Church, pray for me and for all your children who are so deeply in need of the mercy of your Son as it was poured out from the Cross for the redemption of the world. May all your children draw ever closer to you and to your Son, as we gaze upon the glory of the Cross, and as we consume the Most Holy Eucharist. Mother Mary, pray for us. Jesus, I trust in You!

Additional Books in This Series

The *Catholic Daily Reflections Series* is made up of four books covering the entire liturgical year. The books in this series are as follows:

Catholic Daily Reflections Series:

1. *Advent and Christmas*

2. *Lent and Easter*

3. *Ordinary Time: Weeks 1–17*

4. *Ordinary Time: Weeks 18–34*

You may also be interested in our Android and iOS app:

"My Catholic Life!"

Visit our website for more information:

www.mycatholic.life

Printed in Great Britain
by Amazon